Happy Birthday, Grandma Moses

Activities for Special Days
Throughout the Year

Clare Bonfanti Braham and Maria Bonfanti Esche

Illustrations by Mary Jones

CHICAGO REVIEW PRESS

For Bob and Ron, who always believed we could do it.
—M. & C.

Library of Congress Cataloging-in-Publication Data

Braham, Clare Bonfanti.
    Happy birthday, Grandma Moses : activities for special days
throughout the year / Clare Bonfanti Braham and Maria Bonfanti
Esche. — 1st ed.
        p.   cm.
Includes bibliographical references.
    ISBN 1-55652-226-6 : $14.95
    1. Holidays—Juvenile literature. 2. Special days—Juvenile literature.
3. Manners and customs—Juvenile literature.   I. Esche, Maria Bonfanti. II. Title
GT3933.B73   1994
394.2'6—dc20   94-21526
                                                                                                          CIP
                                                                                                          AC

The author and the publisher disclaim all liability incurred in connection with the use
of the information contained in this book.

First edition
Published by Chicago Review Press, Incorporated
814 North Franklin Street, Chicago, Illinois, 60610
Printed in the United States of America
ISBN: 1-55652-226-6

1 2 3 4 5 6 7 8 9 10

DECEMBER

INTRODUCTION

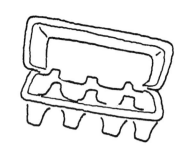

What is there to celebrate in the middle of January?

How about Jakob Grimm's birthday! Take a Hansel and Gretel walk on a cold winter afternoon. A few weeks later, celebrate Chinese New Year with paper dragons, a parade, and Chinese recipes to cook. And go on celebrating—through Native American dry painting in September, to Kwanzaa festivities in December.

The world is our children's neighborhood and Chinese New Year is as much a part of our culture as the Times Square celebration on December 31.

We can learn to bake Hamantashen for Purim as well as cookies for Christmas; we can celebrate Buddha's birthday in April along with Lincoln's in February.

With the many excellent books of children's activities already available, why write or read another? Because we have found no other book that celebrates the many holidays, seasons, and birthdays—January through December—with a global perspective.

Who will use this book? Schools, child care centers, and all those who care for children at home. In fact, anyone who works and plays with children and who would like to spend that time more creatively.

If you didn't realize that June 27 is Helen Keller's birthday and a great time to make and enjoy a "Five Senses Snack," then turn the page and start celebrating! A year's worth of fun and learning awaits you.

Whenever possible we recycle materials to use as our craft supplies. You may want to start collecting the following items:

milk cartons, all sizes

egg cartons

cardboard tubes from bathroom tissue, paper towels, waxed paper

brown paper bags, all sizes

cardboard boxes, all sizes

newspaper, especially colored comics

magazines and catalogs

gardening catalogs

wallpaper sample books (Home decorating stores throw these out as new ones come in. They are often happy to put them aside for you if you pick them up.)

old tickets

cardboard, both thin and corrugated

sandpaper

used computer or printer paper

used gift wrap

Styrofoam meat trays

plastic berry baskets

plastic liquid detergent bottles (dish and laundry)

plastic margarine tubs with lids

coffee cans with plastic lids

plastic lids of all sizes

jars and pill bottles with lids

wooden popsicle sticks

old toothbrushes

old nylon stockings

scraps of fabric, ribbons, lace, old socks, etc.

cotton

scraps of wood, vinyl tiles, carpet

tin cans

corks

buttons

bare branches

In addition, we have used purchased art supplies in many of our projects. These include:

paper and posterboard of all kinds and colors

colored tissue

paints, crayons, and markers

white craft glue

hot glue gun

glitter in assorted colors

JANUARY

"Happy New Year" in Sign Language

HAPPY—Bring right palm up to tap chest twice.

NEW—Both palms up. Back of right hand crosses over left palm twice.

YEAR—Right fist begins on top of left fist, circles left fist and ends back on top (earth revolving around the sun).

Jakob Grimm was born January 4, 1785, and with his brother Wilhelm collected and published many old German folktales, popularly known today as Grimm's fairy tales.

A Hansel and Gretel Walk

You will need:

A loaf of bread (stale bread is fine)

In honor of Jakob Grimm's birthday, read to the children (or have them take turns reading aloud) the story "Hansel and Gretel."

Afterward, taking a loaf of bread with you (stale bread is best), go for a walk. Let the children crumble the bread and drop it on the ground to mark the trail.

When it's time to turn around and go back, is the bread trail still there? If it isn't gone already, reassure the children that the birds will soon enjoy it.

JANUARY 6 | The Epiphany

On January 6, some Christians celebrate the Feast of the Epiphany. This day commemorates the arrival of the three kings (or wise men) who followed a star to Bethlehem to bring precious gifts to the Baby Jesus.

Giving Precious Gifts

You can inspire some lively discussion with older children with a read-aloud of O. Henry's "The Gift of the Magi." Here are some questions to ask:

- What precious gifts do you have to give? We all have some! (They might be your time, talents, listening attention…)
- What would the different people you love—parents, teachers, friends, brothers, sisters—consider a wonderful gift from you?
- What precious gifts have others given you?
- Think of a very precious gift you would like to receive that cannot be wrapped in a package.
- Think of one you would like to give that cannot be wrapped.

A Mitten Tree

You will need:

A large bucket or flowerpot filled with sand
A few tall bare branches

Children of all ages can experience the joy of giving with the following activity.

Fill a large bucket or flowerpot with sand. Then stick tall bare branches in it. Ask the children for a pair of mittens to give to someone who needs them. (Clean used mittens are fine!) You can hang the pairs of mittens on bare branches with clothespins.

Enjoy your colorful mitten tree for awhile. Then deliver your warm gifts to a local charitable organization for distribution.

📖 *The Mitten* by Jan Brett, Putnam, 1989.

Martin Luther King Jr. was born on January 15, 1929. Although he lived less than forty years, he succeeded in making enormous improvements in the lives of African American people. Let us honor his birthday by remembering what a difference this one man made.

Walk Back in Time

Explain to the children:

Not so long ago, when your parents were your age, African American people were not allowed to do many things or go many places just because they had dark skin. Let's try to imagine what it was like to be African American then.

If you were African American:

- At the playground, you couldn't drink from the same water fountain as white children.
- You had to sit in the back of the bus.
- You couldn't use the same bathrooms as white people.
- You could not go to school with white children.
- The water fountains, bathrooms, and schools for you were not as good as those for the white children.

- Your Mom and Dad were not allowed to vote.
- If you were an athlete, you could not play on the same team as white athletes.
- If you went into the Army or Navy, you could not serve in the same units as white people.

In the 1950s and 1960s, a black man named Martin Luther King Jr. worked very hard to change the way it was. He worked for peaceful change in the laws and the way people thought. Because of him, African American people have more equal opportunities today.

On January 15, we celebrate the birthday of Martin Luther King Jr.

My First Martin Luther King Book by Dee Lillegard, Childrens Press, 1987.

A Picture Book of Martin Luther King, Jr. by David Adler, Holiday House, 1989.

You may want to photocopy the following:

"All inhabitants of the globe are now neighbors."

"We have inherited a large house, a great 'world house' in which we have to live together—black and white, Easterner and Westerner, Gentile and Jew, Catholic and Protestant, Moslem and Hindu—a family unduly separated in ideas, culture and interest, who because we can never again live apart, must learn somehow to live with each other in peace."

Martin Luther King Jr.

Born January 17, 1706, Benjamin Franklin is remembered by most of us as a great political statesman and inventor. However, his contributions were so many and varied that he deserves a closer look.

A Picture Book of Benjamin Franklin by David Adler, Holiday House, 1990.

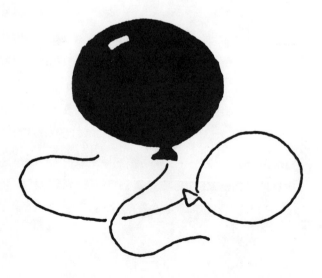

An Electrifying Experiment

Most of us have heard about Ben Franklin's famous kite and key experiment. What this experiment proved was that lightning is electricity. Lightning is caused by natural static electricity in the atmosphere.

The following experiment from *Mr. Wizard's Supermarket Science* (Don Herbert, Random Books, 1980) shows static electricity in action.

You will need:

A few balloons
Unflavored gelatin
Something made of wool (e.g., scarf, sweater, other clothing, etc.)

You may want to work in small groups so that everyone can see.

1. Pour the unflavored gelatin onto a dish.
2. Blow up a balloon and tie it shut.
3. Rub the balloon on the wool. (What you are doing is rubbing electrons from the wool onto the balloon thus producing static electricity.)
4. Touch the area of the balloon that you rubbed to the dish of gelatin. Raise the balloon slowly and watch the gelatin. What happened? Why?

Your "charged" balloon attracted the gelatin. The balloon is charged with static electricity—the same static electricity that Mr. Franklin found in lightning.

It's Fun to Get Mail

You will need:

I envelope for each child
I stamp for each child
A note or drawing done by the child

Ben Franklin was postmaster of the thirteen American colonies. Let's remember him by making use of that postal system he organized more than two hundred years ago.

1. Help each of the children address an envelope with his or her name and home address as the destination. Be sure and put a return address (the child's home, school, or child care facility) on the envelope and explain why a return address is important.
2. Inside the envelope put a picture the child has drawn or a note he or she has written. Then seal it up.

3. If it is convenient, you could visit the post office to buy your stamps and stamp and mail your letters. Explain to the children that the stamp we buy and stick on our letters is how we pay for the service of mail delivery. A stamp is not just a sticker—it is like money. While you are at the post office, look around, and if they aren't busy, talk to the post office employees about their work.

4. If a post office visit isn't possible, stamp your letters and walk to the nearest mailbox to mail them.

5. When your letter arrives, think of Ben Franklin who set up the system so long ago.

You Can Learn Anything at Your Library

Ben Franklin helped to start the first lending library in America. In honor of him, let's pay a visit to the local library.

Many children have been to the public library for story-hour programs and to pick out books to take home. Do they know they can find a book on any subject they are interested in?

Duplicate the call number guide on the following page and give one to each child. Help the children select a subject that interests them and then to find the books on the shelves by call number. Remind them to keep the call number guide and take it along when they visit the library again.

Religion 200's	Myths 292	Money 332	Police 352	Mail Carriers 383	Ships 387.2	Holidays 394.2
Fairy Tales 398.2	Math 510	Stars 523	Electricity 537	Magnets 538	Chemistry 540	Weather 551.5
Rocks 552	Dinosaurs 568	Trees 582	Seashells 594	Insects 595.7	Fish 597	Birds 598
Reptiles 598.1	Mammals 599	Fire fighters 614.84	Trains 625	Airplanes 629.13	Cars 629.2	Space 629.4
Farms 630	Fruit 634	Gardening 635	Pets 636	Food 641	Houses 728	Drawing 741
Crafts 745.5	Music 780	Circus 791.3	Puppets 791.5	Ballet 792.8	Riddles 793.7	Sports 796
Boating 797.1	Poetry 808	Countries 910	Biography B Name	Flags 929.9	Knights 940.1	Native Americans 970.1

Alan Alexander Milne was born in London, England, on January 18, 1882. Although he published many plays, novels, and a detective story, he is best known for his Winnie-the-Pooh stories, which were written for his son, Christopher Robin.

Read aloud from **Winnie-the-Pooh** by A. A. Milne (especially chapters 1 and 2).

Then try the following cookie recipe.

Winnie-the-Pooh's Honey Bears

Have the children blend:

$^1/_2$ cup butter-flavored shortening
$^1/_2$ cup brown sugar
$^1/_2$ cup honey
1 egg

Add dry ingredients:

$2^1/_2$ to 3 cups flour
$^1/_2$ teaspoon baking soda
$^1/_2$ teaspoon salt

Blend well. Dough will be soft. Let the children pat dough flat with their hands on a well-floured surface. Cut out with bear cookie cutters. Bake at 350°F for 5 to 10 minutes. Let cool on baking sheet. Enjoy!

First locate China on a globe or a world map. What countries are China's neighbors? Where is China in relation to your location? What route would you travel to get there?

An exciting holiday for Chinese people all over the world is Chinese New Year, which begins on the first full moon after January 21 and lasts for fifteen days.

The following seven activities work well together as a unit. However, each one can be used alone.

Chinese Greetings

In early January, we learned how to say "Happy New Year" in sign language. Now we can learn a New Year greeting in Chinese.

"Gung Hay Fat Choy" means "Happy New Year" in Chinese. If you meet a Chinese friend when it isn't New Year, you can always say *Ni hao* (Nee how). *Ni hao* means hello!

Chinese New Year by Tricia Brown, Henry Holt, 1987.

Chinese Calendar—
What Animal Are You?

You will need:

Copy of the animals on pages 16 and 17
Scissors
Oaktag or heavy paper
Paint, markers, or crayons
Hole punch
Yarn

In the Chinese calendar, each year is named for an animal. There are twelve animals in the Chinese zodiac. They are the rat, ox, tiger, hare, dragon, snake, horse, sheep, monkey, rooster, dog, and pig. It is believed that a person's personality and character are determined by the animal of the year in which he was born. (Many children can understand this by comparing it to our zodiac signs for each month.)

Below is a calendar that you can use to discover what animal you are! Find your birth year and help the children find theirs. Then look at the descriptions below to see if your personalities match your Chinese zodiac sign.

Year of the:

RAT	1936	1948	1960	1972	1984	1996	2008
OX	1937	1949	1961	1973	1985	1997	2009
TIGER	1938	1950	1962	1974	1986	1998	2010
HARE	1939	1951	1963	1975	1987	1999	2011
DRAGON	1940	1952	1964	1976	1988	2000	2012
SNAKE	1941	1953	1965	1977	1989	2001	2013
HORSE	1942	1954	1966	1978	1990	2002	2014
SHEEP	1943	1955	1967	1979	1991	2003	2015
MONKEY	1944	1956	1968	1980	1992	2004	2016
ROOSTER	1945	1957	1969	1981	1993	2005	2017
DOG	1946	1958	1970	1982	1994	2006	2018
PIG	1947	1959	1971	1983	1995	2007	2019

Born in the year of the:

RAT—You are popular, good at inventing, and very artistic.

OX—You are calm and dependable, a good listener with strong opinions.

TIGER—You are brave, a deep thinker, and courageous in action.

HARE—You are very friendly and talkative. You are trustworthy.

DRAGON—You are very healthy and energetic. You are a considerate friend.

SNAKE—You love good books, good food, music, and plays. You will have good luck with money.

HORSE—You are cheerful, popular, and very complimentary to others. You are a hard worker.

SHEEP—You are very artistic and inquisitive (always asking questions). You are also very wise.

MONKEY—You have a good sense of humor and can always make people laugh. You are good at solving problems.

ROOSTER—You are a deep thinker, a hard worker, and a very talented person.

DOG—You are loyal and good at keeping secrets. You tend to be a worrier.

PIG—You are a very good student and always finish what you start. You are honest and brave.

Copy the animals on the following pages and cut them out. Let the children (or help them) trace their particular animals on oaktag or heavy paper and cut them out. Then ask the children to decorate their animals with paint, markers, crayon, etc.

If you plan to make Chinese paper lanterns, ask the children to sign their animals and give them to you temporarily.

If you are not making lanterns, the children can punch a hole in their animals, slip yarn through, and wear them as necklaces.

Chinese Paper Lanterns

You will need:

Two 9-by-12-inch pieces of construction paper (one red and one yellow)
Scissors
Stapler
Pencil

(Continued on page 18.)

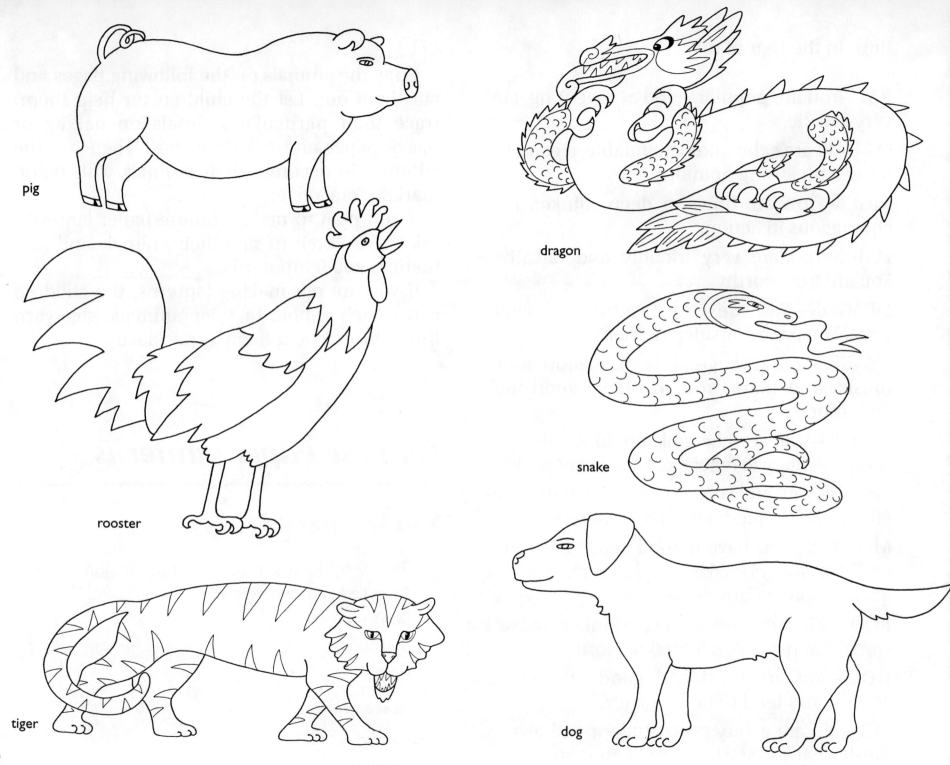

pig

dragon

rooster

snake

tiger

dog

horse

ox

sheep

hare

rat

monkey

17

Have the children:

1. Take two 9-by-12-inch pieces of construction paper, one red and one yellow.
2. The yellow paper is the light inside the lantern. Cut a strip 1 by 12 inches from the yellow paper. Save for later.
3. Roll the remaining 8-by-12-inch yellow paper into a tube 8 inches tall. Overlap about 1 inch and staple into a cylinder shape.
4. The red paper is the outside of your lantern. Red is considered a lucky color in Chinese tradition and is seen a lot at Chinese New Year. Fold the red paper lengthwise in half so that it measures 9 by 6 inches.
5. Cut straight slits about 1 inch apart from the folded edge almost (but not quite) to the cut edge.
6. Open the red paper. Lining up the tops and bottoms, wrap the red paper around the yellow cylinder, and staple the two together.
7. Attach the yellow 1-by-12-inch strip as a handle on top. If you made animals for the Chinese calendar activity, the children can staple their animals to their lanterns.
8. If you are going to do a New Year's Parade, the lanterns look great hung off bare branches and carried carefully in the parade.

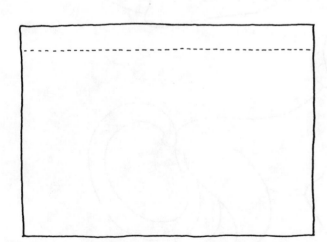 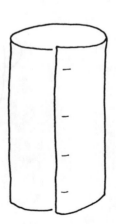 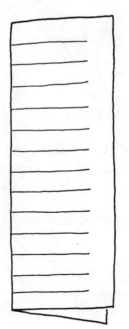 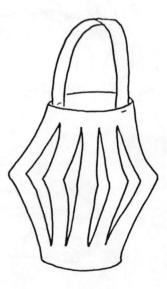

Lion Masks

You will need:

One 9-inch paper plate

Scissors or X-acto knife

Brown and orange paint

Two Styrofoam meat trays

Small pieces of sponge

Red, orange, and yellow tissue paper

Black and red markers

Tongue depressor or craft stick

Stapler

One Chinese New Year tradition is the Lion Dance, performed to "scare away evil spirits and bring good luck for the new year."

Read the following story and then enjoy making your own lion masks with the children.

📖 *Lion Dancer: Ernie Wan's Chinese New Year* by Kate Waters and Madeline Slovenz-Low, Scholastic, 1990.

1. Take a 9-inch paper plate. You (older children can do this themselves) carefully cut the plate with an X-acto knife as illustrated, cutting eye holes and a nose flap. Cut where lines are shown. Cut one plate for each child.

2. Put brown and orange paint out in Styrofoam meat trays. Give each child a small sponge to sponge paint in brown and orange all over the plate. Demonstrate how to just touch the paint-covered sponge to the plate to get a textured effect for the lion's fur.

3. While the paint is still wet, give the children red, orange, and yellow tissue paper. Let them rip strips of tissue about 1 by 9 inches and stick the tissue strips in the wet paint around the circumference of the plate.

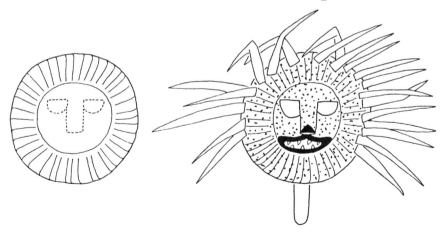

4. When the paint dries, let the children outline the eyes in black marker, add a triangle nose and a lion mouth filled with teeth. Let the children fill in the mouth around the teeth with red marker.
5. Staple a tongue depressor or craft stick to the bottom of the plate as a handle.

Enjoy your Chinese lion mask!

Chinese Dragons

You will need:

Copy of the following illustration
Scissors
Cardboard
Glue
Paint or markers
One 3-by-12-inch piece of construction paper, or two 2-by-36-inch pieces of construction paper
Two tongue depressors or craft sticks
Glue
Stapler
Cardboard
Two tongue depressors or craft sticks

The Chinese New Year celebration ends with the Lantern Festival. On this night, a beautiful giant dragon made of silk and bamboo is paraded along the street. Crowds of people accompany the dragon, lighting his way with paper lanterns.

We can make our own individual dragons for Chinese New Year.

1. Copy the following page, one copy for each child. Let them (or help them) cut out the dragon head, tail, and eyes. Then mount the pieces on cardboard to stiffen them and cut them out again.
2. Let the children use paint or markers to color their dragons in vivid colors.
3. Now you need a body for each dragon. Here are two ideas.
4. Younger children can take a piece of construction paper 3 inches wide and at least 12 inches long. Have them fold the paper back and forth accordion-style. Then they can attach the head (with eyes) and tail to the ends of this body.

21

5. Older children may enjoy making another type of dragon body. Take two strips of different-colored paper 2 by 36 inches (you can tape strips together to achieve the desired length). Hold the strips perpendicular to each other and attach where they overlap with a dab of glue or a staple.

Fold the vertical strip up over the horizontal strip. Then fold the horizontal back over the vertical. Continue folding alternately always toward the junction point until the strips are completely folded. The finished product will look like this:

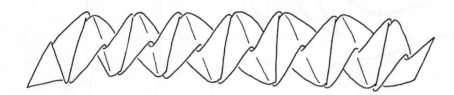

Attach the dragon head (with eyes) and tail to the ends of this body.

6. Whichever body is used, take two tongue depressors or craft sticks and attach one behind the head and one behind the tail. These are the handles. By moving them, you can make your dragon dance!

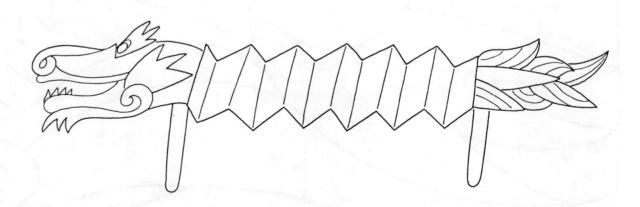

New Year's Parade

No Chinese New Year celebration would be complete without a parade. You can parade around the halls of your school or around your neighborhood. If you have made any of the paper dragons, lanterns, or lion masks, now is a great time to show them off!

Beat drums or rhythm sticks, clash cymbals, and carry a banner wishing "GUNG HAY FAT CHOY" to all you meet!

Chinese Fried Rice— Chopsticks Lesson

Conclude your New Year's celebration with a feast eaten the Chinese way!

Ingredients

1 small bunch green onions
2 eggs
2 to 3 tablespoons oil
3 cups cooked rice
1 cup peas (frozen, fresh, or canned)
1 small can sliced water chestnuts
Soy sauce

1. Chop onions into small pieces.
2. Crack eggs and beat slightly.
3. Heat oil in large frying pan or wok.
4. Add eggs to hot pan and stir continuously.
5. Add rice, onions, peas, and water chestnuts. Add soy sauce to taste, stirring continuously until everything is heated through. This recipe serves 6 children.

When it is time to enjoy your fried rice, explain to the children that in China it is the custom to eat with chopsticks rather than with a fork.

Provide chopsticks for each child. (Chopsticks are available and quite inexpensive at any Asian grocery store.)

 **_Chopsticks! An Owner's Manual_** by Hashi-San, Conari Press, 1991. Hashi-San's book is delightful. It's fun as well as informative. It contains facts about the origins of chopsticks and glimpses into Asian culture.

If you have the time to follow the step-by-step directions, try them. If not, this tip may help. Remember that the bottom chopstick remains fixed at all times. The top chopstick moves up and down to open and close the tips.

Younger children may have too much difficulty with this method, and many Asian restaurants have a helpful trick to make things easier.

Simply take a piece of paper (restaurants use the paper "sleeve" that disposable chopsticks come in) and fold this down into a small wad about ½ inch thick. Place this between the chopsticks about 1 inch from the top. Secure it above and below with a rubber band (make it especially tight on top). This allows the chopsticks to work almost like tweezers.

Cleversticks by Bernard Ashley, Crown, 1991.

Lewis Carroll is the pen name of Charles Lutwidge Dodgson, who was born January 27, 1832. Although a respected mathematician at Oxford University for over twenty years, he is best remembered as the author of *Alice's Adventures in Wonderland* and *Through the Looking Glass.*

A Mad Tea Party

You will need:

1 full sheet of newspaper (about 14 by 22 inches)
Glue
Scraps of paper, streamers, stickers, etc.

For the treats:

Bread and butter
Tea
Sugar, cream, and lemon wedges

A Mad Tea Party seems the perfect way to honor Lewis Carroll's birthday. First, you can all become "hatters" and create your own party hats.

Let each child:

1. Take a full sheet of newspaper and fold it in half.

2. With the folded edge at the top, fold the top two corners down as illustrated here.

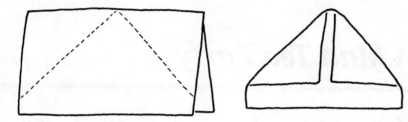

3. Now fold the bottom edge up as far as you can, one paper on each side like a cuff.
4. Pick up the hat by the center of the cuff on each side and stretch it open into a diamond shape.

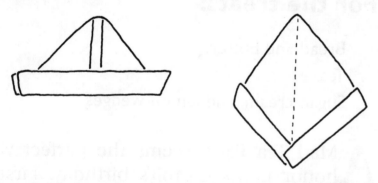

5. Now fold the two open points back (one on each side). The hat should now look like this:

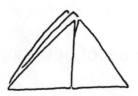

6. Decorate your hat by gluing on scraps of paper, paper streamers, stickers, etc. The crazier the better, because this is your party hat for a Mad Tea Party!

As the glue on the hats dries prepare the tea party.

Let the children make bread and butter sandwiches and cut them into triangle quarters. Prepare pots of tea and cut lemon wedges. Set out a sugar bowl and creamer.

Put on your hats and help the children to tea with cream or lemon and bread and butter.

To complete the celebration, read aloud from:

Alice's Adventures in Wonderland by Lewis Carroll, first published in 1866.

To learn more:

Lewis Carroll: Author of Alice in Wonderland by Carol Greene, Childrens Press, 1992.

February

In 1926 Dr. Carter G. Woodson, an African American historian and educator, established "Negro History Week" as a time to honor African American leaders who were instrumental in the fight for freedom for all black people. He chose to celebrate "Negro History Week" in February because it is the birthday month of both Abraham Lincoln and Frederick Douglass.

Today, the month of February has been set aside as Black History Month, a special time to learn about and remember the many African Americans who have contributed so much throughout our history.

Black History Yesterday

You will need:

    1 coffee can
    1 sheet of plain paper to cover it
    Glue or tape
    Copy of the following list

Take a coffee can and cover the outside with paper. Label it "Black History Makers of Yesterday." Make a copy of the list of names on the following page and cut it into strips, one name per strip. Fold the strips, put them in the can, and let each child pick a name.

Ask the children to research the names they have picked and discover the answer to the question, "How did this person make history?"

For example:

Scott Joplin made history by composing and publishing more than forty pieces of music, including many piano ragtime classics such as "The Maple Leaf Rag" and "The Entertainer."

When the research is done, let each child share his or her information with the group. If a child can't find information on the chosen name, these names can be found in:

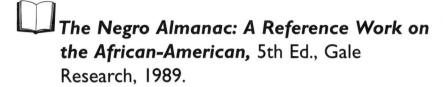 **The Negro Almanac: A Reference Work on the African-American,** 5th Ed., Gale Research, 1989.

Black History Makers of Yesterday

Frederick Douglass	Samuel Kountz
W. E. B. Dubois	Lewis Howard Latimer
Martin Luther King Jr.	Robert H. Lawrence Jr.
Ralph D. Abernathy	Daniel Hale Williams
Malcolm X	Granville T. Woods
Sojourner Truth	Godfrey Cambridge
Harriet Ross Tubman	Nat "King" Cole
Booker T. Washington	Jimi Hendrix
Jackie Robinson	Mahalia Jackson
"Sugar Ray" Robinson	Hattie McDaniel
Gale Sayers	Bill Robinson
Paul Laurence Dunbar	Paul Robeson
Lorraine Hansberry	Ethel Waters
Langston Hughes	William (Count) Basie
Carter G. Woodson	Duke Ellington
Richard Wright	W. C. Handy
George Washington Carver	Billie Holiday
Charles Drew	Scott Joplin

Black History Today

~~~~~~~~~~~~~~~~~~~~~~~~~~~~~~~~~~~~~~~

Set up a bulletin board or wall area labeled "Black History Today." Ask each child to bring in a picture from a newspaper or magazine of a black person making history.

Explain to the children that anyone who works to make a difference in the world is making history. The individuals can be working in any field, i.e., political figures, entertainers, artists, athletes, business people, scientists, doctors, etc.

As the pictures come in, let each child share with the group before hanging the pictures in your "Black History Today" display area. Keep your display up for the month of February.

Will we have an early spring this year or is the worst of winter still ahead? The people of Punxsutawney, Pennsylvania, have an interesting way to predict. Every February 2, these people watch outside the den of a groundhog.

Tradition says that if the groundhog comes out of its den and sees its shadow, it will be frightened and run back inside. If the groundhog does, winter weather will last for six more weeks. However, if the groundhog does not see its shadow, it will stay out and spring-like weather will soon be here. So if you want an early spring, start hoping for clouds on February 2!

We don't have to go to Punxsutawney, Pennsylvania, to see a groundhog come out. We can make our own!

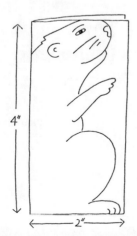

Paper Bag Groundhog

You will need:

> One 9-inch paper plate
> Brown marker, paint, or crayon
> Scissors
> 1 piece of yellow construction paper
> Stapler
> 1 brown paper bag
> Glue
> 1 plastic drinking straw

This craft is especially fun for young children. Have the children:

1. Fold a paper plate in half. This is the hill your groundhog lives under. Color it brown and cut a small hole (about 1 inch) in the middle of the folded side.

2. Our groundhog is coming out on a sunny day. Cut a circle shape about 5 inches in diameter out of yellow paper. This is the sun. Staple it to the back of the hill.

3. Cut a piece about 4 inches square from a brown paper bag. Fold it in half. Draw a simple groundhog (or trace illustration as a pattern) on the folded paper. Cut out but DON'T CUT THE FOLD.

4. Now slip the groundhog over a drinking straw and glue or staple to attach.

5. Open the paper plate and slip the straw into the hole as far as it will go. When the paper plate is closed again, the groundhog is hidden. Push up the straw and the groundhog pops out!

Remember, the sun is shining. Do you think this groundhog will predict an early spring or a long winter?

Silhouettes

You will need:

   I chair
   I large sheet of white paper
   A bright lamp
   Pencils

Older children can take turns helping each other make these shadow portraits.

1. Hang a white sheet of paper on the wall and put a chair in front of the paper. The side of the chair should be facing the paper.

2. One child sits in the chair, and a bright lamp (take off the lampshade) is placed on the side of the child opposite the paper.

3. Adjust the height of the paper until you see the shadow of the child's head on the paper. Move the lamp until the shadow becomes a distinct silhouette.

4. Now another child can trace the outline of the silhouette with pencil on the white paper. (Remind the seated child to stay very still.)

Shadows by Larry Kettelkamp, William Morrow, 1957.

George Herman Ruth (1895–1948), nicknamed "Babe" Ruth, played professional baseball from 1914 to 1936. A talented pitcher, fielder, and hitter, his lifetime record of 714 home runs held until 1974 when it was broken by Hank Aaron.

Henry "Hank" Aaron, born in 1934, began his professional baseball career at age eighteen. At his retirement in 1976, Aaron held the record of 755 home runs.

Both Babe Ruth and Hank Aaron are now in the Baseball Hall of Fame.

Babe Ruth: Home Run Hero by Keith Brandt, Troll Associates, 1989.

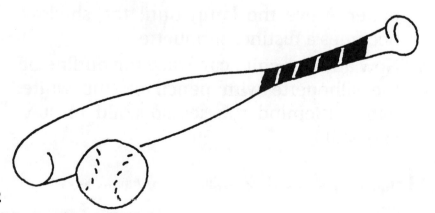

Fun with Baseball

You will need:

Bats

Balls

Tees (construction cones)

Baseball is considered the national sport of the United States. In some parts of the country, spring training begins in February. If the weather in your part of the country is mild enough, celebrate the birthdays of these two great baseball players with a little batting practice. Older children can try to hit pitched balls. Young children can hit off a tee (an orange construction cone makes a good tee).

FEBRUARY 6 | Babe Ruth's Birthday

No matter what the weather, you can get in the baseball mood with a sing-along of this old favorite "Take Me Out to the Ball Game." The song was written in 1908 by Jack Norworth, who created the lyrics, and Albert Von Tilzer, who composed the music.

TAKE ME OUT TO THE BALL GAME

Take me out to the ball game,
Take me out with the crowd.
Buy me some peanuts and Crackerjacks,
I don't care if I never get back.
And it's root, root, root for the home team.
If they don't win it's a shame.
For it's 1, 2, 3 strikes you're out
At the old ball game.

When you are finished, enjoy a snack of roasted peanuts and Crackerjacks!

Born in 1867, Laura Ingalls Wilder grew up in a pioneer family during America's westward expansion. As a woman in her sixties, she began writing a series of children's books describing the day-to-day life of the Ingalls family. Wilder's "Little House" books have given generations of children a vivid picture of life in an earlier America.

For more information about this well-loved American author, read:

Laura Ingalls Wilder: Author of the Little House Books by Carol Greene, Childrens Press, 1990.

Make Your Own Bread and Butter

Read aloud from chapter 1 of *The Little House in the Big Woods* by Laura Ingalls Wilder, Harper & Row, Pub., 1932. Then talk about what all your lives might be like if you lived at the same time and place as the Ingalls family.

What would your house be like? Where would you get furniture and clothes? Who would you play with? What would you do for fun? What kind of food would you eat? Where would you get it?

For Laura Ingalls, even a simple snack like bread and butter became quite a production, requiring time, skill, and effort.

Help the children get a taste of pioneer life as you supervise them in the following cooking project.

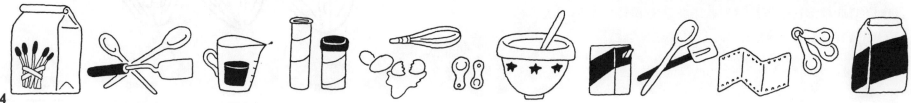

Homemade Bread

Ingredients

1 package (or 2 teaspoons) dry yeast
1½ cups warm water
1 tablespoon brown sugar
1½ teaspoons salt
1 tablespoon butter
4¼ to 4⅓ cups flour
2 teaspoons cornmeal

1. In a large bowl, stir yeast in warm water until it dissolves.
2. Add brown sugar, salt, butter, and 2 cups of flour. Beat with a wooden spoon until thoroughly blended.
3. Gradually add flour until mixture forms a dough that you can handle easily.
4. Knead the dough on a lightly floured surface for 5 to 10 minutes until the dough is smooth and not sticky. (To knead the dough, fold it toward you with the fingers of both hands, then push dough away from you with the heels of your hands.)
5. Place kneaded dough in a greased bowl and cover with a clean cloth. Let dough rise in a warm place until it doubles in size (about 1 hour).
6. When the dough has doubled, punch it down and divide into three or four pieces. Let the children shape these pieces into loaves any shape they choose.
7. Grease cookie sheets and sprinkle with cornmeal. Place loaves on cookie sheets with at least a 2-inch space around each loaf. With a sharp knife, make 3 or 4 slashes in the top of each loaf about ¼ inch deep. Do not cover. Let rise until double (30 to 45 minutes depending on size of loaves).
8. Bake in preheated 375°F oven until golden brown on top (30 minutes or more, depending on the size and shapes of your loaves). Place on cooling racks to cool.

Homemade Butter

You can make this while your bread is baking.

Ingredients

Heavy whipping cream
Small glass jars with lids (one for each 2 or
   3 children)

1. Into each jar, pour 1 to 2 tablespoons of heavy cream. Close the jar tightly.
2. Let the children take turns shaking the cream in the jars vigorously until it becomes solid. You've got butter!
3. When your bread is cool enough to slice, spread it with homemade butter and enjoy!

As you enjoy your snack, ask the children:

- Where would Mrs. Ingalls have gotten the ingredients to make bread and butter?
- Why did we use brown sugar instead of white?
- How would Mrs. Ingalls have baked her bread?
- How would the Ingalls keep their butter cool?

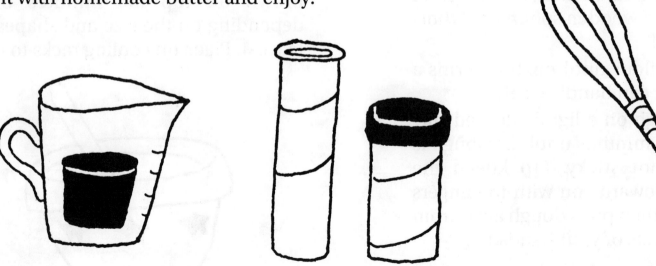

A French custom that has become part of our American tradition, Mardi Gras falls between February 3 and March 9, depending on the date of Easter Sunday.

"Mardi Gras" is French for "Fat Tuesday" and it is the last day before Ash Wednesday, the Christian holy day that begins the six-week Lenten season. In the past, Lent was a time of fasting so "Fat Tuesday" was a day of feasting—a final indulgence before the lean weeks to come. Today there is little fasting in Lent but the tradition of Mardi Gras continues.

Mardi Gras is celebrated in Christian countries all over the world. The biggest celebration in our country takes place in the city of New Orleans, Louisiana. Here an annual carnival brings millions of visitors. There are parades and everyone dresses up in elaborate costumes and masks.

📖 *Mardi Gras!* by Suzanne M. Coil, Macmillan, 1994.

In honor of Mardi Gras, we can make our own masks.

Carnival Masks

You will need:

9-inch paper plates
Hole punch
Six 15-inch lengths of string, two for each mask
Scissors or X-acto knife
Glue

For a Sun Mask you will need:

Yellow paint
Yellow or orange construction paper
White craft glue
Gold glitter

For a Clown Mask you will need:

Crayons or markers
Bright-colored tissue
Bright construction paper
White craft glue
Any color glitter

For a Cat Mask you will need:

Small sponge
Whatever color "cat" paint you want
Construction paper
3 long pipe cleaners
Tape

Have the children:

1. Cut a 9-inch paper plate in half. Punch a hole on each side. Tie a 15-inch string in each hole. Have someone help locate the spots for the eye holes and cut them out. (An X-acto knife works well if you are very careful.) Cut a triangle out between the eyes to fit over your nose.

2. For a Sun Mask:
Paint plate mask bright yellow. Cut tall triangles out of yellow or orange paper. Glue them to the back of the mask around the perimeter like the rays of a sun. Thin a small container of white craft glue with a little water. When the paint on the mask is dry, brush thinned glue all over the mask and rays and sprinkle with gold glitter.

3. To make a Clown Mask:

    Leave the background of the plate white and with crayon or marker draw bright colored triangles above and below the eye holes. Take bright-colored tissue, tear off pieces (roughly 3- to 4-inch squares) and crumple them. Glue an edge of each piece onto the edge of the mask, starting at the string holes and working up. Use a few different colors, if possible. This is the crazy clown hair. Add a triangle of bright construction paper glued to the edge of the mask as a clown hat. Paint the hat with thinned glue and sprinkle with glitter.

4. To make a Cat Mask:

    Paint the plate whatever color you want your cat to be. If you sponge paint, just touching the paint-dipped sponge to the paper in a dabbing technique gives a nice "furry" texture. Cut out triangle ears from construction paper and add to the back edge of the plate when the paint is dry. Take three pipe cleaners and cut them in half. With clear tape, attach them to the mask on either side of the nose hole for whiskers.

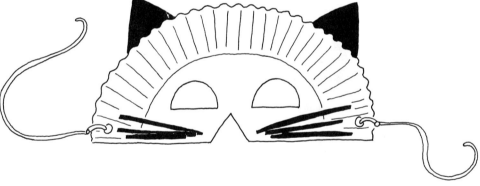

These suggestions are a starting place. Children often have their own wonderfully creative ideas. Just provide a lot of interesting craft supplies: paint, sequins, glitter, pipe cleaners, cotton, colored paper and tissue—then stand back! (Or get going on your own mask.)

Thomas Alva Edison was born February 11, 1847. He had only three months of formal education but he became famous throughout the world for his many inventions (he patented over a thousand!) including an automatic telegraph system, the phonograph, the incandescent electric lightbulb, and the kinetoscope, forerunner of the motion picture camera. He even invented waxed paper!

A Lesson on Light

You will need:

- Candle
- Oil lamp
- Lamp with bulb
- Copy of the following page
- One 12-by-18-inch sheet of black paper
- Piece of yellow construction paper
- Scissors
- Glue
- Old magazines
- Gold glitter

One of Edison's many inventions was the electric light bulb. In honor of his birthday, talk about light with the children.

Bring in a candle, an oil lamp, and a lamp with an incandescent bulb. Darken the room and light only the candle. Talk about the limits of candlelight. Light the oil lamp and blow out the candle. Is the light better? Now turn on the lamp and blow out the oil lamp. How does this light compare with the other two? Now light up the room for a project.

1. Copy the following page (lightbulb), one copy for each child.
2. Give each child a 12-by-18-inch sheet of black paper.
3. Let the children cut out the large bulb shape and glue it on the middle of the black paper (hold the black paper so that it is 18 inches long and 12 inches across). Trace the small base shape on yellow paper, cut it out and glue it on the bottom of the bulb.
4. Give the children old magazines and have them cut or tear out pictures of lights (lamps, flashlights, car headlights, street lights, lighted signs—anything that uses electric light). Let them glue their pictures inside their bulb shapes.
5. Finally, let the children write "Happy Birthday, Thomas Edison" across the top and bottom of their paper in glue. Then cover the glue with gold glitter. Lay pictures flat until they are dry.

Making a Recording

You will need:

Tape recorder
Blank tape

As the inventor of the phonograph, Thomas Edison was the first to record voices. Using a tape recorder and microphone (a children's Fisher-Price tape recorder with built-in microphone works great), record the children's voices. Do an interview program or your own "talk show," and make sure that every child says a few sentences.

When you play back your recording, are you surprised at how your voice sounds?

This opportunity to hear yourself as others hear you was brought to you by Thomas Edison!

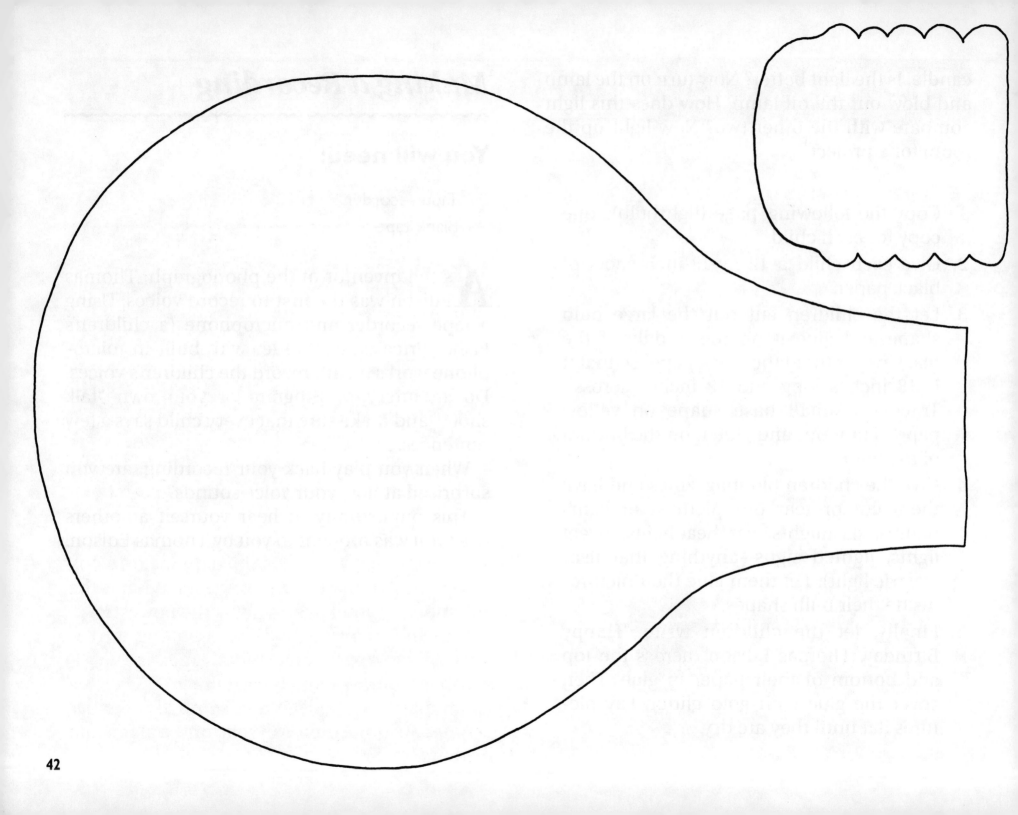

FEBRUARY 12 | Abraham Lincoln's Birthday

Abraham Lincoln, our sixteenth president, was born on February 12, 1809, in a log cabin in Kentucky.

📖 *A Picture Book of Abraham Lincoln* by David Adler, Holiday House, 1989.

The following three activities are fun ways to remember this great man.

Shining Pennies

You will need:

Lots of pennies
Jar with lid
Dish detergent
$1/2$ cup white vinegar
3 tablespoons salt

Bring in a lot of pennies (the duller the better) and let the children take a good look at them.

Look at the front. Whose face is on the penny? What else is on it? What do the words say? What do they mean? What does the date mean? Look for pennies for many different years. What is the oldest penny you have? What is the newest?

Turn the penny over. What building is pictured? Read the words. What language is "E Pluribus Unum"? What does it mean?

You may have noticed that some of the older pennies are quite dull. Will soap and water shine them up?

Let the children:

Fill a jar with water and a little dish detergent. Add some dull pennies. Close the lid and shake the jar well. Open the jar and check your pennies. Are they shiny (not just wet)?

Explain to the children that pennies are made of copper and when copper gets old it gets tarnished. It takes a special solution to remove tarnish.

Let the children:

Rinse the jar clean. Pour ½ cup of white vinegar into the jar. Add 3 tablespoons salt. Add some dull pennies. Close the lid and shake the jar well. Open the jar and check the pennies. Are they shiny now? Be sure to rinse the pennies well. Save the shiny pennies for the next activity.

Pitching Pennies into Lincoln's Hat

You will need:

Picture of Lincoln in his stovepipe hat
2- or 3-liter plastic soda bottle
Scissors
12-by-18-inch black posterboard
Glue or tape
Circle of black posterboard, 8 inches in diameter
Pennies

Show the children a picture of Lincoln in his "stovepipe" hat. Why is it called a "stovepipe" hat?

Make a stovepipe hat to play this game. If you have a big group, you can make a few of these.

1. Cut the top off a 2- or 3-liter plastic soda bottle, leaving a plastic cylinder shape about 8 inches tall.

2. Take a 12-by-18-inch piece of black paper and cut it, leaving it 18 inches long but just wide enough to cover the bottle's height. Wrap it around the bottle and glue to attach.

3. Cut a circle of black posterboard large enough so that when you place your cylinder on it a couple of inches of cardboard show all around. (For a 2-liter bottle, make a circle 7½ inches in diameter.) This is the hat brim.

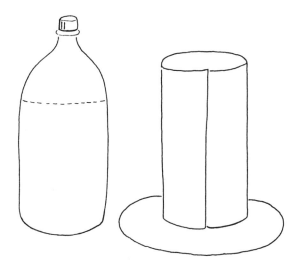

4. Glue the bottom of the paper-covered bottle to the cardboard circle. You have an open-topped stovepipe hat!
5. Put the hat on the floor. Tape a line on the floor at an appropriate distance from the hat. Now give each child 5 shiny pennies to try to pitch into Lincoln's hat. If there is time, give everyone a few turns.

Penny Rubbings

You will need:

Lightweight paper
Crayons or markers
Pencil
Pennies

1. Give each child a sheet of not too heavy paper. Computer paper or lightweight typing or drawing paper is fine.
2. Across the top of the paper, have the children print "HAPPY BIRTHDAY, ABRAHAM LINCOLN!" in crayon or marker.
3. Give each child a sharpened pencil and a few pennies and show them how to make "rubbings" of the pennies. They can make designs or patterns if they like. Make sure they try rubbing both the fronts and the backs of their pennies. Try pressing heavily and lightly with the pencil. Try using the point or the flat side. Which technique do they like best?

FEBRUARY IS HEART MONTH

Valentines aren't the only hearts we think about in February. Since a presidential proclamation in 1964, February has been National Heart Month in the United States.

Sponsored by the American Heart Association, National Heart Month is a time to learn more about our hearts and how to keep them healthy.

Listen to Your Heart

You will need:

Stethoscope

Using a stethoscope, help the children listen to their hearts. After everyone has heard his or her "resting heart rate," get moving!

Spend 5 to 10 minutes jogging, skipping rope, doing jumping jacks, etc. Stop the children one by one to listen to their heart rate. How does it compare to the first time they listened? Let the children walk around the room for a few minutes to cool down gradually.

Talk about the fact that our heart is a muscle, and like any other muscle our hearts need exercise to get strong and healthy. Talk about aerobic exercise, i.e., exercise that makes the heart and lungs use more oxygen (makes us breathe harder). Can the children think of any aerobic exercises? (Walking, jogging, running, biking, swimming, and jumping rope are all examples.)

Explain to the children that 20 minutes of aerobic exercise 3 to 5 times a week can help keep their hearts healthy.

Eating for a Healthy Heart

Exercise is important for healthy hearts and so is eating right. Eating for a healthy heart means eating lots of fruits, vegetables, and whole grains and eating limited amounts of protein and fat.

Talk about these guidelines in a way children can understand. Which is healthier—french fries or carrot sticks? An apple or an ice cream cone?

Some foods taste so good we can still enjoy them for an occasional treat but it's fun to try new recipes that are delicious and good for our hearts, too!

Orange Fruit Cups

3 large oranges
1 banana, sliced
1 cup seedless grapes (sliced lengthwise)
2 kiwi, peeled and sliced

Cut oranges in half and scoop orange sections out of skin. Break orange sections into bite-sized pieces and mix with sliced bananas, grapes, and kiwi. Divide fruit into 6 portions and serve in orange halves.

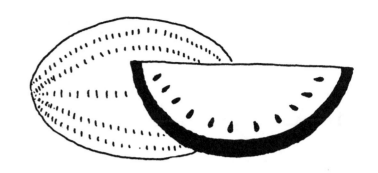

Taking good care of yourself with regular exercise and nutritious food is one way of saying "I Love You" to the people who care about you. Here is another way.

"I Love You" in Sign Language

Here are two ways to say "I Love You" in sign language.

I—Point your index finger to your chest.

LOVE—Using "A" hands, cross your arms across your chest crossing at the wrist, palms toward body (as if you are holding something precious to you).

YOU—Point index finger straight ahead.

Here's a simple way:

Hold the hand with little finger, index finger, and thumb extended in front of your chest. (I Love You.)

"I Love You"

Today is the anniversary of the birth in 1902 of one of the world's greatest singers. Starting as a little girl in a church choir in Philadelphia, Marian Anderson grew up to sing for kings, queens, and presidents all over the world. However, at the same time Anderson was enjoying enormous success in Europe, she was forbidden from appearing in America's best concert halls simply because she was African American. But nothing could stop her reputation from growing, and in 1955, Marian Anderson became the first African American singer to appear with the Metropolitan Opera.

Listen to a recording of Marian Anderson.

Sing a Spiritual

The first songs Marian Anderson ever performed were hymns and spirituals, and even when she was a world famous concert artist, she always included spirituals in her repertoire. Black spirituals are a style of music unique to African American culture. After they were brought to this country as slaves, many African Americans adopted the Christian religion of their owners. The hymns they sang reflected the hardships of their lives here on earth and their hopes for a better life in heaven. This theme of God's goodness runs through all black spirituals.

You can celebrate the birthday of this great American by learning and singing a black spiritual. The following spiritual was sung often by Marian Anderson throughout her career.

HE'S GOT THE WHOLE WORLD
IN HIS HANDS

The song is 150 years old, though it was first published in 1927.

He's got the whole world in His hands,
He's got the whole world in His hands,
He's got the whole world in His hands,
He's got the whole world in His hands.
He's got the itty bitty baby in His hands,
(three times)
He's got the whole world in His hands.
He's got you and me brother in His hands,
(three times)
He's got the whole world in His hands.
He's got you and me sister in His hands,
(three times)
He's got the whole world in His hands.
He's got the whole world in His hands,
(four times)

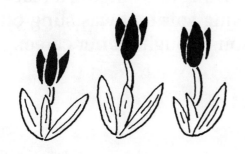

The Polish astronomer Nicolaus Copernicus was born February 19, 1473. Sometimes called "The Father of Modern Astronomy," Copernicus introduced the theories that the planets revolve around the sun and that the Earth spins on an axis, completing one rotation per day. Before the Copernican system was published in 1543, the Earth was thought to be the center of the universe.

To honor the birthday of this great astronomer, we can make:

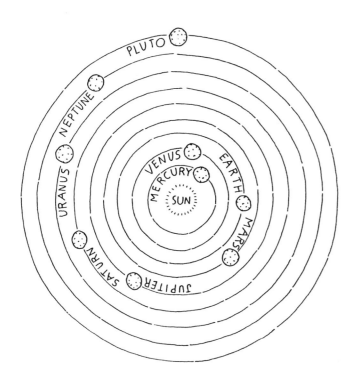

The Copernican Universe

You will need:

Circle compass
Drawing paper
Markers or crayons
Brass paper fastener
18 "dot" stickers

Read the following book aloud to the children:

📖 ***The Magic School Bus Lost in the Solar System*** by Joanna Cole, Scholastic, 1990.

Explain to the children how Copernicus changed our idea of the universe, then work together to make each child a model of Copernicus's sun-centered system.

1. Using circle compasses, let (or help) the children make ten concentric circles of gradually increasing size. The first (smallest) should be yellow. This circle represents the sun. The other nine circles represent the orbits of the nine planets.

2. Have the children write "sun" on the yellow circle. On the edge of each of the other circles, from smallest to largest, have (or help) the children write Mercury, Venus, Earth, Mars, Jupiter, Saturn, Uranus, Neptune, and Pluto respectively.

   This might be a good time to teach the children an easy way to remember the order of the planets with respect to the sun. *My Very Excellent Mother Just Served Us Nine Pizzas.*

   Take the first letter of each word in the sentence. These stand for the nine planets in order, starting with the planet closest to the sun. Very rarely, Neptune replaces Pluto as the farthest planet; most of the time the order of the planets is: MERCURY—VENUS—EARTH—MARS—JUPITER—SATURN—URANUS—NEPTUNE—PLUTO.

3. Have the children fasten the circles one on top of the other in descending order by poking a brass paper fastener through the center of the sun and all the other circles.

4. Remind the children that except for the "sun" in the center, these circles represent the orbits of the planets circling the sun.

5. To represent the planets, give each child 18 dot stickers. They should stick these dots (sticky sides together) to the edge of each circle, one dot "planet" for each orbit, next to each planet's name.

   Now spin the orbits and watch your planets revolve around the sun, just as Copernicus said they did over 400 years ago!

   Remind the children that although our model is two dimensional, the universe is three dimensional with planets orbiting the sun on all different planes.

George Washington was born on February 22, 1732. Virginia planter, Commander-in-Chief of the American army in the Revolutionary War, and first president of the United States of America, Washington truly earned the nickname "the Father of our Country."

Read the following biography of George Washington aloud. Then enjoy the activities that commemorate George Washington's birthday.

📖 *A Picture Book of George Washington* by David A. Adler, Holiday House, 1989.

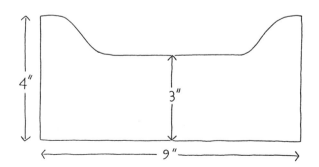

Tricorn Hats

You will need:

Oaktag or cardboard
Copy of the following illustration
Stapler
Scissors
Small pieces of red, white, and blue paper

Show the children a picture of Washington wearing a colonial tricorn hat. We can make our own hats like General Washington's.

1. On cardboard or oaktag make a pattern according to the illustration below.

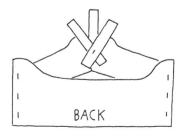

2. Cut out the pattern three times and staple the three pieces together at side edges, about 1 inch from the edge. Now you have a triangle shape.

3. Add an American cockade to the hat. Cut one red, one white, and one blue rectangle (about $4\frac{1}{2}$ inches long by 1 inch wide). Staple them to the front panel of your hat as illustrated.

Design Your Own Dollar

You will need:

$1 bill
Drawing paper about 9 by 4 inches
Crayons or markers

Show the children a dollar bill. Who is on the front? Look at the images of the Great Seal on the back. After the children have looked carefully at the dollar, give each child a piece of paper about 9 by 4 inches.

Let them design their own United States dollar. In pictures and in words the children can put what they think deserves to represent America on our money. Using markers or crayons in any color they choose, let the children design both front and back of their dollars.

Your Presidential Proclamation

You will need:

Copy of the following illustration
Markers or crayons

Our president does not govern alone but works in cooperation with Congress to pass our laws. However, once in a while, the president uses his power to make changes by "Presidential Proclamation."

Ask the children to imagine that each of them is president. "You have the power to make one change by presidential proclamation. What will you proclaim?"

Proclamations can be silly (pizza proclaimed as the national food, your birthday as a national holiday) or serious (anyone caught polluting will have to spend at least one year working in an environmental clean-up program).

Copy the presidential proclamation form on the following page, one for each child. Children should fill in their names and proclamations and illustrate them if they like. Then share them with the group.

I, _____
President of the United States
of America,
do hereby proclaim _____

_____

_____

_____

_____

MARCH

PURIM—THE FEAST OF LOTS

The joyful Jewish holiday of Purim falls in February or March on the fourteenth day of the Hebrew month of Adar. It originated more than 2,500 years ago.

The history behind Purim can be found in the Book of Esther of the Bible, and Jewish people read this story on the holiday. It tells of King Ahasuerus of Persia (now Iran), his good Queen Esther, and a wicked man named Haman. The evil Haman made a plan to kill all the Jewish people. Queen Esther, who was Jewish herself, successfully pleaded with the King, stopped Haman, and saved her people.

A good children's book to read aloud is:

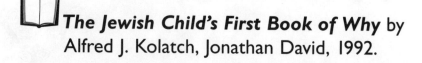 **The Jewish Child's First Book of Why** by Alfred J. Kolatch, Jonathan David, 1992.

Then celebrate this happiest of Jewish holidays by baking the following traditional treat.

Hamantashen

These traditional three-cornered pastries are shaped to resemble the three-cornered prime minister's hat worn by evil Prince Haman.

2/3 cup margarine or butter	2 1/2 to 3 cups sifted unbleached flour
1/2 cup sugar	1 teaspoon baking powder
1 egg	Dash of salt
1/2 teaspoon vanilla	1 can poppy seed or nut filling

1. Cream the margarine and sugar together. Add egg and continue creaming until smooth.

2. Add vanilla. Stir in flour, baking powder, and salt until a ball of dough is formed.

3. Chill 2 to 3 hours or overnight.

4. Preheat oven to 375°F.

5. Roll out about one-fourth of the dough at a time onto a lightly floured board to a thickness of one-eighth inch. Cut with a glass into 2-inch circles. With your finger, wet the rim of the circle with water. Fill with 1 teaspoon poppy seed or nut filling and fold into three-cornered cookies. (Press left edge, right edge, and folded edge toward you all into the center and press the edges together, like a tricorn hat sealed together in the center.)

6. Bake on a well-greased cookie sheet 10 to 15 minutes or until the tops are golden.

Pocahontas was a Native American princess who lived in Virginia in the beginning of the 1600s, when the English established the settlement of Jamestown. Legend tells us that Pocahontas saved the life of one of these settlers, Captain John Smith, who was about to be executed by her father, Chief Powhatan. We know as fact that Pocahontas married an Englishman, John Rolfe, and by this marriage secured peace between the Native Americans and the English for several years. Pocahontas went to England with her husband and their son and died there of smallpox in 1617.

Many North American Indian maidens wore feathered headbands as part of their traditional dress. We can remember this brave Indian princess with the following activity.

Indian Headbands

You will need:

Brown paper bag
Construction paper in an assortment of colors
Scissors
Pencil
Markers or crayons
Glue
Stapler
Tape

Let each child:

1. Cut a 2-by-24-inch strip of paper from a brown grocery bag.
2. Trace and cut out two circles from contrasting colors of construction paper—one about 3½ inches in diameter and one about 3 inches across.

3. Trace and cut out 3 simple feather shapes about 7 inches long and 2 inches wide from three different colors of construction paper. Cut a ³/₄-inch fringe on both sides of each feather by cutting at a downward angle.

4. Glue the feathers onto the larger colored circle, stems together, feathers fanning outward. Next glue the smaller circle, on top of the larger circle, centering it. (The feathers are secured between the two circles.) Let dry.

5. Decorate the brown headband with simple Indian symbols drawn in crayon or marker. You can draw simple pine trees, canoes, stick figures, birds, sun, waves (curving lines), corn, deer.

6. Staple the headband to fit. Cover staple with a piece of tape.

7. Staple your mounted feathers onto the headboards so that they are centered on your forehead.

A good juvenile biography is:

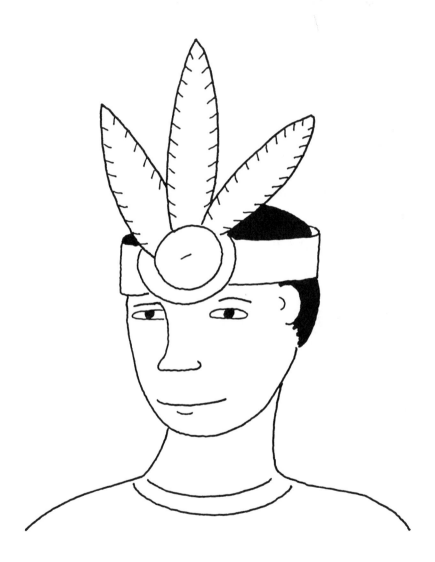

Pocahontas: Daughter of a Chief, Carol Greene, Childrens Press, 1988.

Theodor Seuss Geisel was born on March 2, 1904. Writing under the pen name Dr. Seuss, Geisel revolutionized children's literature with his zany and highly original books beginning with *And To Think That I Saw It On Mulberry Street*, published in 1937. Some of his characters, including the irreverent "Cat in the Hat" and grouchy "Grinch," have become a part of our culture.

Green Eggs á la Dr. Seuss

Celebrate Dr. Seuss's birthday with a read-aloud of one of his classics, then the following recipe.

 **Green Eggs and Ham** by Dr. Seuss, Beginner Books, a division of Random House, 1960.

You will need:

Eggs
Milk
Green food coloring
Butter or margarine

Let the children take turns cracking eggs into a big bowl. Add a little milk and take turns beating with a fork or wire whisk. Finally, add a few drops of green food coloring and beat to blend in color.

Cook your eggs in butter or margarine. Then give each child a sample.

Encourage all the children to try at least a taste. Remember the story; we can't say we don't like something until we give it a try.

Talk about trying new foods, especially foods that might look strange to us. Remind the children that even if we don't care for a food, we shouldn't laugh at or make fun of someone else's food. The food that seems so strange to us is perfectly delicious to someone else.

MARCH 3 Alexander Graham Bell's Birthday

Alexander Graham Bell was born on March 3, 1847 in Scotland. As a man he moved to the United States and worked as a teacher of the deaf in Boston, Massachusetts. While working on a machine to help the deaf in 1876 he invented the telephone. Today, thanks to Alexander Graham Bell, we can talk to people all over the world without leaving home!

Making Telephones

You will need:

2 empty tin cans

Awl

Hammer

String or ribbon at least 36 inches long

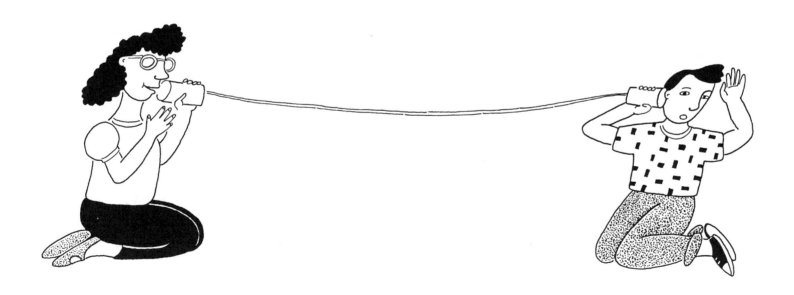

In honor of Alexander Graham Bell's birthday, let's invent our own telephones. It's fun to work in pairs for this activity.

1. Give each child an empty tin can (about 1 pound size works well). Check to make sure there are no rough edges on the rim.

2. Using an awl and a hammer, let each child carefully punch a small hole in the bottom of each can.

3. Give each pair of children a string or ribbon at least 36 inches long. Let the children make a knot at one end of the string and then thread the string through the hole in one can and then the other, knotting the other end of the string so it won't slip through the hole.

4. Now the children are ready to talk to each other. One child should hold one can to his ear and pull gently until the string is taut. The other child should talk in a soft voice into the other can. The voice should travel along the string into the cans and into your ears! Take turns talking and listening.

Musical Telephone Numbers

You will need:

Index cards
Pencil

It isn't always easy for young children to remember their phone numbers, but it is extremely important to know, especially in case of an emergency. Here's a fun way to learn.

Write each child's phone number on an index card and give it to him or her. Now sit in a circle with the children. One at a time, let each child hold up the index card and as they do, all sing the following song, substituting the numbers and name of each child.

Sing to the tune of "Happy Birthday":
FIVE-FIVE-FIVE-OH-NINE-ONE-ONE
FIVE-FIVE-FIVE-OH-NINE-ONE-ONE
IF YOU WANT TO CALL LAURA
FIVE-FIVE-FIVE-OH-NINE-ONE-ONE

Emergency Telephone Skills

Using the telephone can be fun when we're talking to friends but it can be a lifesaver in an emergency.

Talk about when to call the emergency number: when the grown-up who takes care of you is hurt or seems to be asleep and can't be awakened.

Ask the children to imagine and talk about specific emergency situations. Talk about how to call your local emergency number. (Practice on a real phone that is not plugged in or on a toy telephone.)

Remind the children when making a real telephone call to listen first for a dial tone.

Try to get stickers from the police department with the local emergency number on them and give one to each child. These should be displayed on or near their home telephones.

Remind the children that if they make an emergency phone call, they should not hang up until the grown-up on the other end tells them to.

Important: Emphasize that we never call the emergency number as a joke. That is against the law.

First locate Ireland on a globe or world map. What countries are Ireland's neighbors? Where is Ireland in relation to your location? What route might you travel to get there?

In America, we celebrate St. Patrick's Day on March 17 by wearing green and watching parades, but in Ireland, March 17 is much more important. Ireland: National Day is a national legal holiday recognized by the government and honored throughout the country.

The following three "Irish" activities can help us to celebrate the day.

An Irish Greeting

Although almost all of the people of Ireland speak English today, the traditional language of Ireland is Gaelic. Gaelic is still a required subject in all state-supported schools in Ireland.

A traditional Gaelic greeting on St. Patrick's Day is Erin Go Bragh (pronounced ERIN GO BRAH). Erin is another name for Ireland and Erin Go Bragh has been translated as "Ireland Go Free," or "Ireland Forever."

Irish Potatoes

Potatoes are an important crop in Ireland. In fact, when the potato crop failed in the mid-1800s, there was a terrible famine that sent many Irish emigrating to new lands, including America.

The following recipe is really for delicious candy. It only looks like potatoes!

Irish Potato Candy
Ingredients

- 1 pound box plus ½ cup powdered sugar
- 4 ounces (1 stick) margarine
- 1 teaspoon vanilla
- 3 to 5 tablespoons cream
- 1 cup coconut
- 1 tablespoon cinnamon

Mix together the first 4 ingredients, saving ½ cup of the powdered sugar for later. Add coconut and mix well.

Roll into little balls. Put on tray. Dry in the air for 1 hour.

Mix ½ cup powdered sugar and cinnamon together. Shake balls and cinnamon mixture in a plastic bag to coat the balls. Makes about 75 Irish potatoes.

Irish Soda Bread

This is a traditional Irish bread that uses baking soda and buttermilk instead of yeast as leavening.

Ingredients

- 4 cups flour
- 1 teaspoon salt
- 1 tablespoon baking powder
- 1 teaspoon baking soda
- ¼ cup sugar
- 2 cups raisins
- ¼ cup butter or margarine, softened
- 1 egg
- 1 ¾ cups buttermilk

Combine flour, salt, baking powder, baking soda, sugar, and raisins in a large bowl. Add butter or margarine and cut in with a pastry cutter (or two knives) until crumbly. Mix slightly beaten egg with buttermilk and add to flour mixture. Stir until blended.

Turn dough onto a floured surface and knead for 2 to 3 minutes until smooth.

Grease two round 8-inch cake or pie pans. Preheat oven to 375°F. Divide dough in half and shape each half in a round loaf. Put the loaves into the pans and press the dough down until it fills the pan. With a sharp knife, cut a cross into the top of each loaf (about ½ inch deep).

Bake for 35 to 40 minutes. Bread is delicious warm or cold, buttered or plain.

On this day, the sun crosses the equator in its apparent movement from south to north. On the vernal equinox, day and night are equal in length, and in the Northern Hemisphere the vernal equinox signals the beginning of spring.

If March 21 brings spring where you live, you may enjoy the following three activities.

"Spring" in Sign Language

Right hand begins with fingertips touching the thumb, all pointed upward like a closed flower just breaking through the ground. Right hand in this position pushes through the left hand, which is in "C" position, facing the right.

As right hand pushes through left hand, fingers of right hand spread up and out as it moves up (a flower sprouting up and opening). Repeat.

Lion and Lamb Bag Puppets

To make a Lion Puppet you will need:

Brown paper grocery bag

Scissors

Markers or crayons

2 plastic "googly" eyes

Craft glue

Brown lunch bag

To make a Lamb Puppet you will need:

White lunch bag

Copy of the following illustration

Scissors

Black construction paper

Pencil

Craft glue

Cotton balls

Markers or crayons

2 plastic "googly" eyes

It is often said that if March comes in "like a lion" with rough and blustery weather, it is sure to go out "like a lamb" with mild, gentle weather.

Talk about this old saying with the children, then make lion and lamb puppets out of lunch bags.

Lion Puppet

1. Let the children cut a circle about 8 inches in diameter from a brown paper bag. Cut fringe about 1 inch long all around the edge of the circle. This is your lion's mane. Inside the circle add your lion's face—triangle ears, a long diamond-shaped nose, a mouth, and whiskers. For your lion's eyes, add two plastic "googly" eyes (sold in craft supply stores).

2. Glue your lion's head to the bottom panel of a brown lunch bag.

Lamb Puppet

1. Start with a white lunch bag (available in most craft supply stores).

2. Copy the lamb's head on the following page and cut it out. Let the children trace it on black construction paper and cut it out.

3. Spread glue across the top of the head (not the ears) and stick on cotton balls. Add "googly" plastic eyes and draw nostrils with black marker.

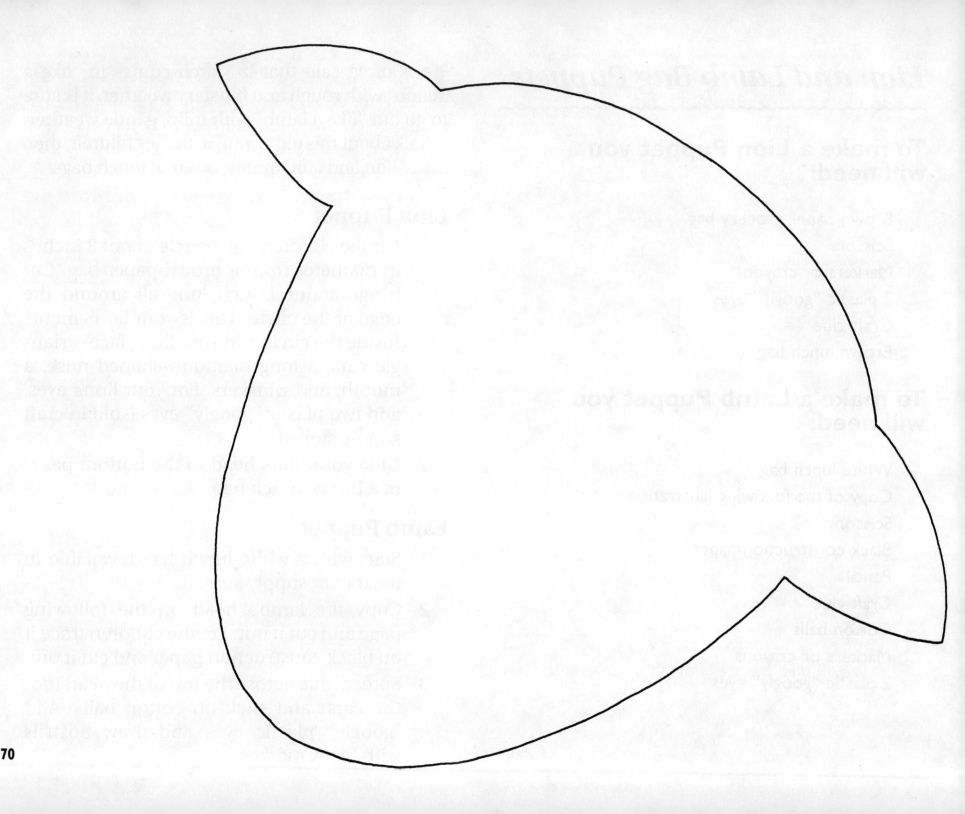

4. Now glue your lamb's head to the bottom panel of the white lunch bag.

Wind Streamers

You will need:

Tongue depressor or craft stick

Three 12-inch pieces of different-colored crepe
 paper

Stapler

This is an outside activity. Give each child a tongue depressor and put out a few rolls of different-colored crepe paper. Let each child choose three colors of crepe paper and cut or tear off one piece of each about 12 inches long. Staple the three pieces together to the top of the tongue depressor. Then go outside and let the children run holding up their wind streamers. Notice how the wind moves the crepe paper.

Randolph Caldecott was born in Chester, England, on March 22, 1846. Interested in drawing even as a boy, he grew up to become famous as a book illustrator and is, in fact, credited with originating the children's picture book.

The Caldecott Medal is an award given every year to honor the artist who illustrated the finest picture book of the year. The medal was named for Randolph Caldecott since he was the person who established the picture book as a part of children's literature.

Enjoy a Caldecott Winner

The children's librarian at your community or school library can get you a list of the books that have won the Caldecott Medal through the years. Get as many as you can at the library and display them on a table or bookshelf in your room. Invite the children to browse through them and enjoy the beautiful illustrations.

Talk about what these books all have in common. Explain that the award they won is not for the stories but for the pictures. Explain what an illustrator does and that although sometimes the author and illustrator of a book are the same person, they often are not.

Finally, choose one or two Caldecott Medal winners to read aloud to the children. The following are some of our favorites. The name following the title is the illustrator.

1948   ***White Snow, Bright Snow,*** DuVoisin
(Lothrop)

1963   ***The Snowy Day,*** Keats (Viking)

1964   ***Where the Wild Things Are,*** Sendak
(Harper)

1968   ***Drummer Hoff,*** Emberly (Simon &
Schuster, original publisher Prentice Hall)

1970   ***Sylvester and the Magic Pebble,*** Steig
(Windmill/Simon & Schuster)

1976   ***Why Mosquitoes Buzz in People's
Ears,*** Dillons (Dial)

1980   ***Ox-Cart Man,*** Cooney (Viking)

1986   ***The Polar Express,*** Van Allsburg
(Houghton Mifflin)

1988   ***Owl Moon,*** Schoenherr (Philomel)

MARCH 30 | Vincent van Gogh's Birthday

Vincent van Gogh was born in the Netherlands on March 30, 1853. Although he only painted for ten years, he produced more than eight hundred paintings and changed the world of art forever. Among his most famous paintings are his many *Sunflowers*, his self-portraits, and *Starry Night*.

You might enjoy looking at the following series:

van Gogh by Mike Venezia, Getting to Know the World's Greatest Artists Series, Childrens Press, 1988.

Sunflower Mosaic

You will need:

Copy of van Gogh's *Sunflowers*
9-by-12-inch corrugated cardboard
Pencil
Different-colored dried beans and seeds
Craft glue
Paint brushes or craft sticks

Display some prints (or art books opened to the prints) of van Gogh's *Sunflower* paintings.

Point out to the children the vivid colors and thickly textured paint (he applied it with a palette knife). Can they see the brush strokes?

Now draw a simple outline of a "van Gogh" sunflower for the children to see.

Give each child a piece of corrugated cardboard about 9 by 12 inches.

Let them draw the outline of a large, simple sunflower shape on the cardboard. (Encourage them to keep it large and simple because small details don't show up well with this technique.)

Then put out containers, each with a different-colored bean or seed.

Examples of different-colored beans and seeds:

yellow—popcorn

red—pinto or kidney beans, lentils

green—split peas

black—black beans

tan—lentils

beige—barley, navy beans, limas

Let the children spread craft glue with paint brushes or craft sticks on their designs *one section at a time.*

Then fill in each section completely with beans or seeds. Finally, fill in the background with a contrasting color bean or seed. When the seed mosaics are dry, display them.

Some designs that may not be clear up close look wonderful when viewed from a few feet away.

APRIL

INTERNATIONAL CHILDREN'S BOOK DAY

On this day in 1805, Hans Christian Andersen was born in Denmark. A poor boy, Andersen grew up to travel the world and publish poetry, plays, novels, and travel books. He became famous, however, for his many wonderful fairy tales, including "The Snow Queen," "The Little Mermaid," "The Ugly Duckling," and "The Emperor's New Clothes." Andersen's fairy tales are a beloved part of children's literature throughout the world.

Hans Christian Andersen's birthday has been chosen to be International Children's Book Day. Today, when the world is our neighborhood, tales from around the world can help us understand and appreciate many cultures and customs different from our own.

Advertise Your Favorite Book

You will need:

Large sheet of paper or posterboard
Crayons or markers

Give the children some time to think about their favorite books. Encourage them to show these books to you and to other children participating in this activity.

Give each child a large sheet of paper or poster board and some crayons or markers. Have each child make a poster advertising his or her favorite book. Each poster should include the title and author and an illustration—perhaps some favorite characters or a great scene from the story.

When the posters are finished, display them and let each child tell what makes the chosen book so special. You might want to finish celebrating International Children's Book Day by reading aloud your favorite Hans Christian Andersen fairy tale. You have more than 150 to choose from. Explain to the children that these stories have come all the way from Denmark to delight children and grown-ups here in America.

In 1948, the World Health Organization (WHO) established World Health Day as a time to talk about health around the world. World Health Day looks at a new health topic every year.

The following activity helps us to celebrate World Health Day and learn good hygiene at the same time.

Tissue Craft

You will need:

9-inch paper plate

Crayons or markers

Sheet of drawing paper

Scissors

1 tissue

Glue

Pencil

Good hygiene is one important way to stay healthy. Very young children can be taught:

When you cough or sneeze,
Think of others, please.
Cover your mouth!

Making the following craft is a fun way to remember.

1. Give each child a 9-inch paper plate and crayons or markers, then draw a face to fill the paper plate.

2. Next, let or help each child trace one hand on a piece of paper and cut out the hand.

3. Give each child one tissue to glue to the hand, then attach the hand and tissue to the paper plate, covering the nose/mouth area of the plate.

4. Hang the plates to remind the children that covering our noses and mouths when we cough or sneeze stops the spread of germs and promotes good health.

Germs Make Me Sick! by Melvin Berger, Harper & Row, 1985.

APRIL 8 Buddha's Birthday

First locate the continent of Asia on a globe or world map. What countries make up the continent of Asia? Where is Asia in relation to your location? What route might you travel to get there?

There are over 250 million members of the Buddhist religion today. Most of them live in China, Japan, Korea, and Southeast Asia. On April 8, many of these people celebrate a birthday of the founder of their religion, Siddhartha Gautama, known as Buddha, or the enlightened one.

Buddha lived in India about 2,500 years ago. He did not teach about God, but about how to live a good life and how to understand yourself. After he died, Buddha's followers organized his teachings into a new religion.

In Japan, Buddha's birthday is also called the Flower Festival. At this time of year, Japan's beautiful cherry trees come into bloom and hundreds of Buddhist temples, shrines to Buddha, are covered with flowers.

In honor of this Japanese tradition, we can create our own flowers using the Japanese art of paper folding—origami!

Origami Flower

You will need:

8-inch square sheet of paper (origami or wrapping paper)

1. Give each child a square sheet of paper about 8 inches across. You can buy special origami paper in most craft stores, which comes in beautiful vivid colors. However, any crisp paper will work, even giftwrap.
2. Have the children hold the paper like a diamond and fold the bottom half up to make a triangle.

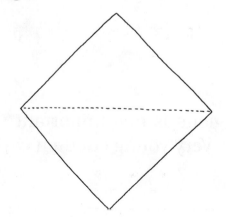

3. Fold this triangle in half to mark the center line and then unfold.

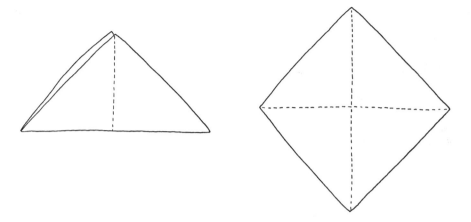

Your finished flower looks like this:

4. Fold outer corners upwards.

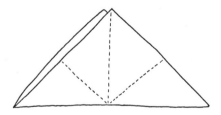

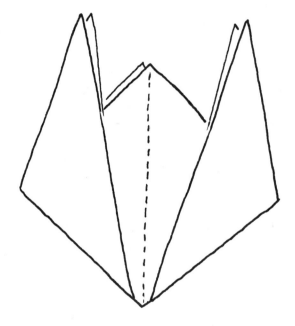

The **Complete Book of Origami** by Robert J. Lang, Dover, 1988.

APRIL 15 — Leonardo da Vinci's Birthday

The term "Renaissance man," meaning a person who has many different talents, certainly could have been created for Leonardo da Vinci. Born in 1452 in Florence, Italy, he lived to be a masterful painter, sculptor, musician, engineer, architect, scientist, and mathematician.

📖 *da Vinci* by Mike Venezia, Getting to Know the World's Greatest Artists Series, Childrens Press, 1989.

Explain to the children that a portrait is a painting of a person. Among da Vinci's many celebrated paintings is one of the most famous portraits in the world today, *La Gioconda* also known as the Mona Lisa.

Find a print of the Mona Lisa to show the children. What do they think of it? Why do they think it is still so famous almost five hundred years after it was painted?

Now let's try our hands at portrait painting!

Paint a Portrait

You will need:

Mirror
Drawing paper
Pencil
Paints
Paintbrushes

Give each child paper, pencils, and paints.

Our portraits will be self-portraits—something famous artists have often painted because their model is as close as their mirror and always available!

The children will need mirrors. A full-length mirror turned horizontally can serve several children at once.

Let the children make a quick sketch of their faces. Don't spend too much time drawing; this is a painting project.

Remind the children that to be true portrait artists they must learn to really look. Don't just draw an oval face because you think faces should be oval. Look—what shape is your face? Round, heart-shaped? Is it wide or narrow?

Look at every feature in this way. Where are your eyes in relation to your face—one-third of the way down? Halfway down? Are they far apart or close together?

This is an exercise in *seeing* more than painting. If we've really seen our faces more clearly, then our portrait is a success, even if it never hangs in a museum!

Earth Day was first celebrated in the United States on April 22, 1970. Senator Gaylord Nelson of Wisconsin worked to set aside a day to teach Americans how to live with respect for their planet. He worked with other concerned people to organize Earth Day and the day was a great success.

More than twenty million Americans participated! On April 22, 1990, the second Earth Day was celebrated. This time more than 200 million people around the world participated. Since then, every April 22 is recognized as Earth Day.

The following book is a wonderful introduction to this special day.

Earth Day by Linda Lowery, Carolrhoda Books, 1991.

Clean-up Walk

You will need:

Gloves
At least 5 trash bags
Antibacterial soap

A clean-up walk is a rewarding experience for children of any age. Environmental problems can seem so overwhelming that it is good to do something with tangible, positive results.

Before you go out, make sure there are gloves for everyone and at least five trash bags (you'll probably need and want more). The five bags are to separate:

1. Glass (*Be careful!*)
2. Cans
3. Recyclable paper and cardboard
4. Recyclable plastic (Check for the recycle symbol on the bottom.)
5. Nonrecyclable garbage

You may choose to clean up a field, a playground, or an area in your neighborhood. We know of one school that had a clean-up of the school playground, including a contest between the boys and the girls to see who could collect the most trash. How many bags can you fill up?

Remind the children that leaves, twigs, pine cones, etc. are not trash. In fact, they can recycle themselves into new earth without our help.

If you come upon any hazardous waste (chemicals, batteries, oil, paint, etc.) tell the children that only an adult should touch it. Be careful handling it and dispose of it responsibly.

When you finish your clean-up walk, dispose of your nonrecyclable trash, and recycle what you can.

Even though you wore gloves, everyone should wash hands with antibacterial soap.

Now give yourselves a round of applause. You really made a difference for our planet today!

Even very young children can enjoy the following book.

It's My Earth, Too by Kathleen Krull, Doubleday, 1992.

Keeping Our Air Clean

Go outside with the children and everyone take some big deep breaths. What does the air smell like? What does the sky look like? Is the air clear or hazy?

In some large cities, the air is so polluted that going outside and breathing can actually make you sick. But breathing is something everybody has to do every minute of every day to stay alive. So what can we do to keep our air clean? Talk about it.

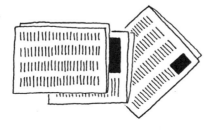

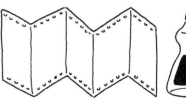

Think before you get in that car! Cars and trucks are a big source of air pollution. If you can walk or bike to where you are going, leave the car at home. Or take a bus; one bus can take a lot more people than a car.

If you must drive, drive smart! Carpool. If you and your friends are all going to the same place, ride together. Talk to your parents about carpooling to work and school. Instead of taking ten separate trips, combine your errands into one trip, and give the Earth a break!

Every single person can make a big difference when it comes to keeping our air clean.

What happens to all our garbage after the garbage truck takes it away? Share this startling fact with the children (from Al Gore's *Earth in the Balance*, Houghton Mifflin, 1992). "Fresh Kills Landfill in New York receives 44 million pounds of garbage every single day. At this rate, it will soon become the highest point on the Eastern Seaboard south of Maine."

No one wants to see our Earth turn into a giant garbage dump, but what can we do to stop it?

Reduce, Reuse, Recycle

Reduce—Reuse—Recycle in the Classroom

You will need:

Large cardboard carton

Pencil

Piece of cardboard

Markers or crayons

Scissors

Sheet of newspaper (comics)

Glue

Talk about ways to reduce the garbage you produce at school. When you are using paper, make sure you use both sides.

Bring your lunch in a reusable container instead of a bag that gets thrown away. Use a thermos instead of a disposable juice box.

If a toy breaks or a game or book gets torn, don't throw it out, fix it! And when you finally must dispose of something, really *think:* Can this be recycled?

If your community has a recycling center, try to visit it. See what kinds of material can be recycled. How is it separated? How much of the trash picked up in your community is recycled?

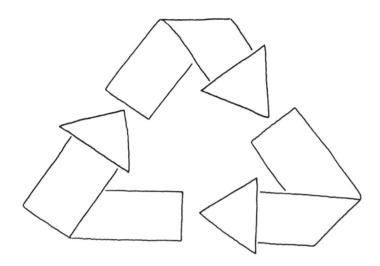

Look at the recycle symbol. What do the arrows mean? Now go back and try the following project.

Classrooms use a lot of paper. Work together to make some recycling containers for paper and cardboard.

Most recycling centers separate newspaper, cardboard, and other paper. If you have a large group, you can break into three smaller groups and make one container for each.

1. Get a large cardboard carton for each group.
2. Have the children make an arrow pattern by tracing a 12-inch ruler on a piece of cardboard and drawing a triangular arrowhead on the top. Cut it out and let the children use the arrow as a pattern.

3. Let each child trace three arrows onto newspaper (colored comics are fun), and cut them out.
4. Display a large recycle symbol for all the children to look at. Show them how to fold over each arrow to duplicate the symbol.
5. When their arrows are folded, let them glue their recycle symbols all over their recycling boxes.
6. Now label the boxes for newspaper, cardboard, or other paper. Find a place for them in the room and fill them up. *Remember: Each 4-foot stack of recycled newspaper saves the equivalent of one 40-foot pine tree!*

Reduce—Reuse—Recycle at Home

You will need:

Empty liquid laundry detergent bottle
  (64 ounce)
Construction paper
Scissors
Glue
Markers or crayons

Talk about ways to reduce garbage at home.

Buy food with the least possible packaging. Those single-serving microwave meals or snacks are fun but they make a lot of garbage. When you go food shopping, encourage Mom and Dad to buy giant economy size—just one box for all that food.

Set your table with china or plastic dishes, not paper, and use cloth napkins.

When you outgrow your clothes or toys, don't throw them out, pass them on to someone smaller.

Some things are actually dangerous to put in the regular garbage. One such hazardous waste product is old household batteries. In a landfill, the chemicals in the batteries can leak out and seep into our groundwater.

When batteries don't work anymore, here's a way to dispose of them safely.

1. Give every child a clean, empty liquid laundry detergent bottle. Some have an inner spout. If it does, reach in and pull it out.
2. Give the children construction paper to cover the labels on both sides of their bottles. Let them cut the paper to fit.
3. Before gluing the paper over the labels, the children should use crayon or marker to draw the following: a large recycle symbol with the words "All Dead Batteries" within the symbol. (You draw it large and show it to them.)
4. Have the children attach the two papers to the front and back of the bottles and take their battery recycling jugs home. When anyone needs to throw out a dead battery, throw it in the jug. When the jug is full, take it to the closest hazardous waste disposal site, empty it, and bring it home to use again.

Born on April 23, 1564, in Stratford-on-Avon, William Shakespeare lived to become the greatest English playwright. The thirty-eight plays he wrote fall into three categories—comedies (e.g., *A Midsummer Night's Dream*, *As You Like It*, *The Taming of the Shrew*), tragedies (e.g., *Hamlet*, *Othello*, *Macbeth*, *King Lear*), and histories (e.g., *Julius Caesar*, *Henry IV*, *Richard II*).

Shakespeare died on April 23, 1616, but his name will live forever through his plays and sonnets. To learn more about him, read:

The Bard of Avon: The Story of William Shakespeare by Diane Stanley and Peter Vennema, Morrow Junior Books, 1992.

Although the text of this book is a little advanced for young children, it is well worth summarizing, and the illustrations alone are a wonderful introduction to the theater of Shakespeare's England.

"A Play's the Thing"

What better way to celebrate William Shakespeare's birthday than by putting on a play!

Young children may enjoy dramatizing a favorite fairy tale or nursery rhyme. Don't worry about memorizing lines, just let the children ad lib according to the context of the story. Wear simple costumes from your dress-up box.

For more ideas, browse through the following book.

Children's Plays From Favorite Stories: Royalty-free Dramatization of Fables by Sylvia E. Kamerman, Boston Plays, 1959.

Older children can enjoy improvising if they are given the "bare bones" of a situation and some simple props. Your library is sure to have some books with great ideas for improvisation. Look under nonfiction call number J812 for more ideas.

Be a Set Designer

You will need:

Shoe box

Old magazines or catalogs

Glue

Scissors

Crayons or markers

Clay, dollhouse furniture, action figures, rocks, sand, twigs, etc.

Colored paper or fabric

It takes more than actors to put on a play. People work as costume designers, lighting specialists, and, to create the scene, set designers. Using shoe boxes, let the children make dioramas depicting a stage set for a play.

1. First, encourage the children to think about the play they want to stage in their shoe box theater. Does it take place outside or inside? If outside, what kind of landscape—forest, meadow, seashore, mountains, etc.? If inside, what kind of room—living room, kitchen, bedroom, office, restaurant, castle, etc.?

2. You don't have to be a great artist to produce the backdrops. You can certainly draw a scene but you can also cut out pictures from magazines or catalogs. Holding the shoe box on its side, decorate the back and sides of the box.

   Then color the bottom inside "floor" of the stage to look like ground, beach, grass, carpet, etc.

3. Now it's time to set the stage with furnishings. Again, you can certainly create your own furnishings from cardboard or clay, but you can also make use of dollhouse furniture, Legos, action figure props, etc. For an outside scene, you can use stones, rocks, twigs, sand, etc.

4. Finally, out of colored paper or fabric, cut a curtain to frame the stage and glue or staple it on. Your stage is set—on with the show!

Arbor Day is a day set aside in April every year in honor of trees. The first Arbor Day was celebrated in the United States on April 10, 1872 in Nebraska. On that day more than one million trees were planted in Nebraska. Today, most states in the United States, as well as Canada and Israel, celebrate Arbor Days.

The Giving Tree by Shel Silverstein, Harper & Row, 1964.

Forests—Using Them vs. Using Them Up

Prepare in advance a bag or box of products of the forest that do not require the destruction of our forests.

You will need:

Good things to eat like nuts (brazil, pecans, cashews, almonds, chestnuts, walnuts), honey, spices (vanilla, allspice, cloves, nutmeg), fruit (avocado, bananas, guava, mangoes, papaya), maple syrup, chewing gum (chicle, the base for chewing gum, is made from tree sap)

A medicine bottle (One out of four medicines in the drugstore originated in a tropical rain forest.)

Eucalyptus throat lozenges or *ointment*

A life-preserver (the stuffing is kapok, from the pod of a tree)

Rubber bands or a *rubber tire*

Include an "empty" jar—it's actually full of air (Trees absorb CO_2, produce O_2, and forests counteract the effects of global warming.)

A bottle of water (like sponges, forests soak up water and reduce its evaporation), a container of dirt (forests prevent soil erosion)

An umbrella, not to keep you dry but to use as a parasol (trees give us shade, cutting down the need for air conditioning)

Include some stuffed animals or *pictures of animals:* raccoons, rabbits, squirrels, many kinds of birds, monkeys, jaguars, tigers, etc. (The forest is home for all of these.)

If it looks like you'll need a pretty huge bag, you've got the right idea!

Ask the children to share as many uses of the forest as they can think of. Write their suggestions on a blackboard or chart. Solicit all the ideas you can without commenting on any of them at this point. When the children have shared all their ideas, stop writing and start talking.

Explain that our forests are a natural resource and just like oil, coal, water, etc., they are not unlimited; they can be used up. We can always plant more trees but it takes hundreds of years to replace a forest.

Now take another look at your list of forest uses and put a star next to the ones that make use of the forests without using them up. Our forests are much more than just a source of lumber, but some of the things our forests provide are not always easy to see.

Pull out your forest products one by one and talk about them with the children. We think the children will never take forests for granted again!

The Rain Forest

You will need:

Bulletin board or poster

Large paper "trees" to cover the poster

Copy of the following illustrations

Markers or crayons

Scissors

Stapler or tape

A rain forest is a particular kind of forest in which between 70 and 150 inches of rain fall each year. This special moist environment makes the rain forest one of the richest communities of life on earth. Covering about 6 percent of the earth's surface, the rain forest is home to $2/3$ of all the species of plants and animals in the world.

When we hear the word "forest" we think of trees, but it is important to understand that a forest is a lot more than just trees.

The following activity is a "hands-on" way to show the children just what a rain forest is.

1. First prepare a bulletin board or big poster by attaching cut-out paper trees to the background. You can make very simple trees—just make sure they are big and tall and there are a lot of them. *Be sure to cover the background completely with trees.*

2. Now copy the two pages of illustrations that follow so you have enough for each child to get one or more animal or plant.

3. The children can color and cut out their forest plants and animals.

4. Before the coloring and cutting is done, tell the children to notice the names of their plants and animals. When they have finished cutting and coloring, call out each plant and animal name one at a time saying (for example):

"The rain forest is a home for *jaguars.*"

Then all the children with jaguars can come up and staple or tape their animals into the forest. Point out the fox and the spotted owl to the children when they come up. These animals live in our own American rain forest. Although most of the rain forests are in the tropics, we have a temperate rain forest in our Pacific Northwest between northern California and Alaska.

toucan

macaw

heliconius (passion flower) butterfly

howler monkey

iguana

tree frog

jaguar

pygmy marmoset

94

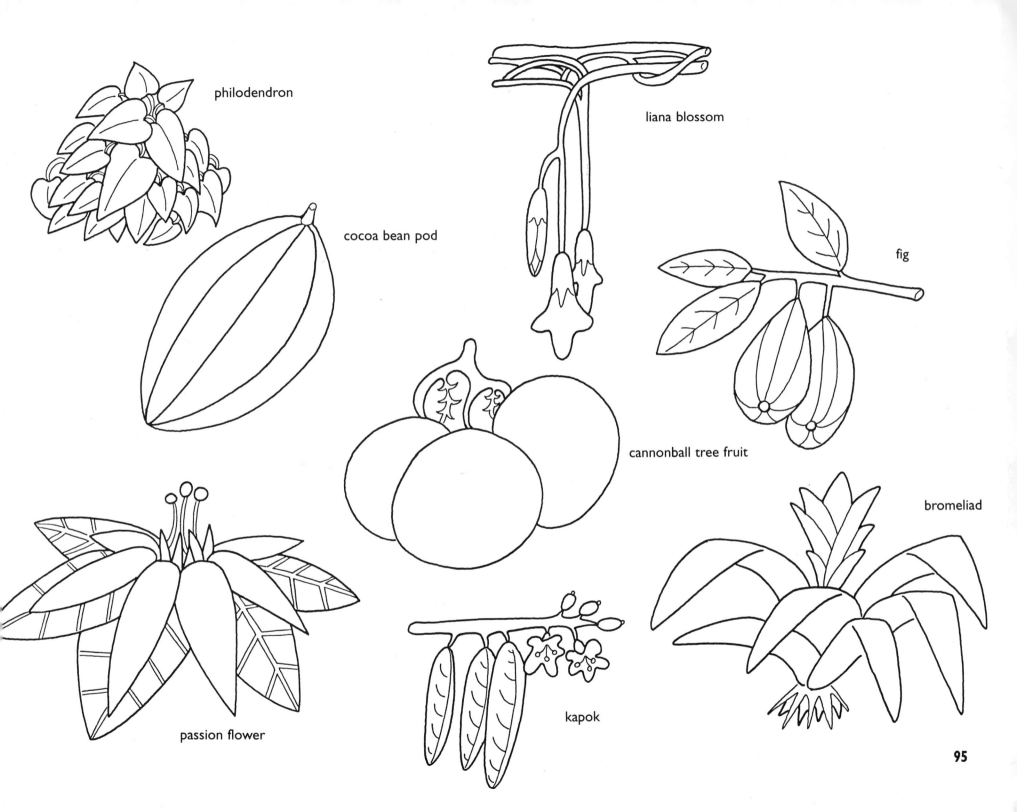

philodendron

liana blossom

cocoa bean pod

fig

cannonball tree fruit

bromeliad

passion flower

kapok

95

5. When all the animals and plants are in the forest, tell the children: Today rain forests are being cut down at the rate of about 100 acres every minute! What do you think happens to all the animals and plants that live there when the forests are cut down, since many can't live anywhere else.

6. Pull the trees off the background. What happens to the animals and plants attached to the forest?

In fact, today one plant or animal species disappears forever every hour! What can we do to stop this? How can we save the rain forest?

The rain forests are being destroyed for many different reasons. Here are just a few of these reasons along with some suggestions to help save the rain forest.

1. Some people cut down the rain forest to use the land as pasture for cattle. They raise the cattle for beef and sell the beef to the United States and other countries where a lot of beef is used to make fast-food hamburgers. The saddest thing is that rain forest land is not good pasture land and after just a few years, it has to be abandoned.

What can you do?

Find out which fast-food restaurants in your area use beef from cattle raised on old rain forest land. (Your reference librarian can get you the address of the corporate office where you can write for this information.) Do not buy food at these restaurants. If enough people do this, the restaurants will get the idea and find another place to get their beef.

2. Sometimes the rain forests are cut down for lumber.

What can you do about it?

Spread the word among friends and families not to buy products made from teak, mahogany, ebony, and rosewood—all wood from rain forest trees. If enough people stopped buying products made from this wood, it wouldn't be worth it for people to chop down the trees.

3. Instead of buying products that come from destruction of the rain forests, buy products that make use of the rain forest without using it up, for example, cashews, brazil nuts, tropical fruits.

This helps the people who live in rain forest areas to earn a living without destroying the rain forests.

And remember, celebrate Arbor Day all year. Take care of the trees we have and plant more wherever there is space for them.

An excellent reference book with more information on this subject is:

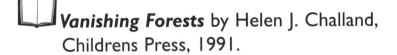 *Vanishing Forests* by Helen J. Challand, Childrens Press, 1991.

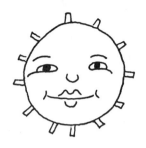

APRIL 26 | John J. Audubon's Birthday

John James Audubon was born April 26, 1785, in Santo Domingo (now Haiti). He studied art in France, returned to America, and became a naturalist. He was especially interested in drawing birds!

In 1838, Audubon published *The Birds of America*, in which more than a thousand birds were beautifully and accurately illustrated life-size. Today an internationally respected conservation group is named for this great naturalist—The National Audubon Society.

Get a copy of Audubon's *The Birds of America* and let the children enjoy looking at the beautiful illustrations.

Bird Watching— Look and Listen

Take the children outside on a bird-watching expedition. (No matter where you live, city or country, you can find birds.) Remind the children that they need to be still when they see a bird or they will scare it away.

Be patient and look and listen carefully. Do you hear any bird songs? Can you identify any? If possible, bring some binoculars so that you can get a closer look at any birds you see. It's also fun to bring a field guide so you can try to identify the birds you spot. There are many excellent field guides. Here's one suggestion:

Birds of North America by Chandler S. Robbins, Bertel Bruun, and Herbert S. Zim, Golden Press, 1966.

Making Flying Birds

You will need:

Copy of the following illustration
Cardboard
Scissors
Craft glue
Any color felt
Fabric paint in squeeze bottles
Needle and thread

With felt and some glue, we can create our own flying birds.

1. Copy the bird outline that follows. Cut it out, glue it to cardboard, and cut it out again. Let the children use it as a pattern.
2. Let each child pick out a color of felt and trace the bird pattern twice on the same color. Cut out the two bird shapes.

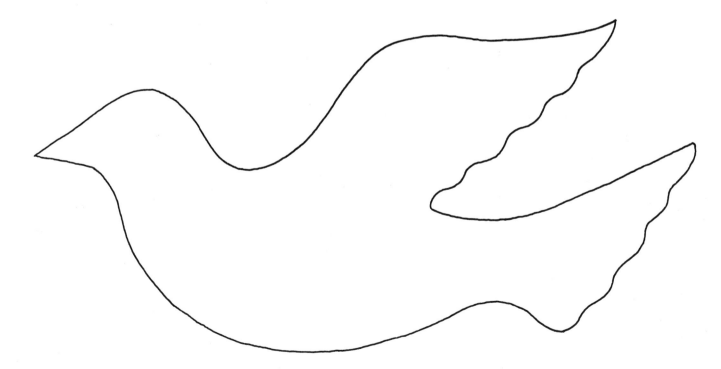

3. Lay the bird shapes down next to each other, beak to beak. Using fabric paint in squeeze bottles (available in craft stores), decorate the bird's head, body, and tail (not wings) on just this side (don't turn them over yet). Decorate as much or little as you like; the sky's the limit.

4. When the paint is completely dry, turn the two birds over to the unpainted sides and decorate only the wings. Let dry completely.

5. Using craft glue, glue the head, body, and tail (*not the wings*) of your two birds, so that the painted bodies face out on both sides. Let dry.

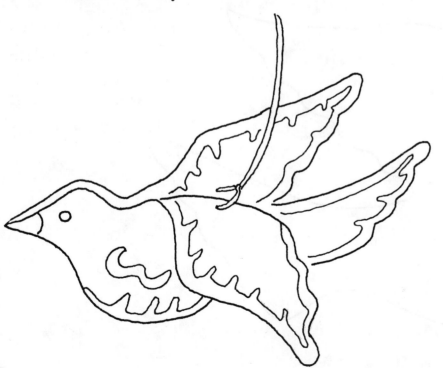

6. When you hold your bird by the body, his pretty wings flap down. You can hang your birds by taking a large stitch with a needle and thread across the top of the wings. Before knotting the thread, try a few stitches to find the center of gravity so that your bird will hang evenly and not slant upwards or nosedive!

Building a Nesting Box

You will need:

2 empty clean half-gallon milk cartons

Serrated-edge knife

Pencil or pen

Stapler

Scissors

Weather-proof paint or Contact paper

18 inches twine

In some parts of the world, April is the time many birds build their nests. If birds are nesting in your neighborhood, you can help by building this nesting box.

1. Each child needs 2 empty clean half-gallon milk or juice cartons.

2. Take the first carton and cut it about 6¹/₂ inches up from the bottom (a serrated-edge knife works well but be very careful!). Discard the top part of the carton. Using a pencil or pen, poke 5 or 6 drainage holes in the bottom of the cut carton. Put this aside.

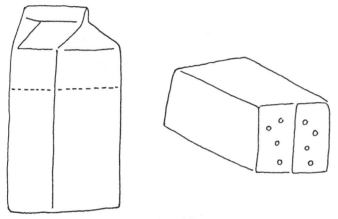

3. Take your second carton and staple the spout shut. Next cut off just the very bottom of the carton. Now push the cut carton from step 2 into the second carton. This makes a stronger nesting box than a single carton would.

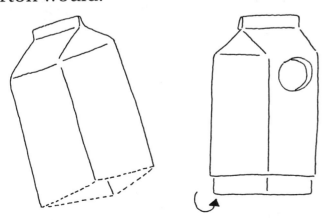

4. Trace a circle about 1¹/₂ inches in diameter on one side of the carton near the top. Cut out the circle (both the outer and inner cartons must be cut).

5. At this point, if you like, you can paint the carton with weatherproof paint or cover with Contact paper.

6. You will need an adult's help with this part. Poke two holes at the top of the carton. Thread a piece of heavy string or twine through the holes. You will use the twine to hang your nesting box.

7. Hang the nesting box outside in a shady spot—the milk cartons get too hot for the birds if they are hung in the sun. Try to hang it in a place where you can see the birds building their nests without being so close that they will be frightened away. If you're lucky, you may even see a new family emerge in a few weeks!

Write to the Audubon Society

It's fun to watch the birds and when we offer them food, water, and nesting areas, they give us in return the pleasure of their company.

For more ideas on how to create a refuge for the birds in their own backyards, let the children write to:

The National Audubon Society
645 Pennsylvania Avenue, S.E.
Washington, D.C. 20003

Describe the neighborhood you live in (urban, suburban, rural), and the experts at the Audubon Society can give you some advice on how to make birds more welcome there.

MAY

The Mother Goose Society of Melrose Park, Pennsylvania, has declared May 1 to be "Mother Goose Day." In honor of the day, enjoy some old favorites from the following book.

The Real Mother Goose, Checkerboard, 1991.

Jack Be Nimble Jumping Fun

You will need:

Small unbreakable candlestick
Unlit candle

Put a small unbreakable candlestick with an unlit candle in it on the floor. Let the children take turns one by one jumping over the candlestick as you all say the nursery rhyme aloud.

The Real Humpty Dumpty

You will need:

Several blocks to make a "wall"
Shallow pan
Raw egg
Markers

ook at a picture of Humpty Dumpty. Do the children realize that he was an egg?

Work together to build a small "wall" (6 to 12 inches tall) of blocks on a table. At the base of the wall place a shallow pan.

Now take a raw egg and carefully draw a face on it. Hold the egg so that it is "sitting" on the wall.

Together recite the Humpty Dumpty nursery rhyme and let your Humpty Dumpty "have a great fall" into the pan. The children really love to watch this dramatization so feel free to do it again—four more times! You can use the five eggs you've cracked for the following activity.

Pat-a-Cakes

arefully remove the eggshells from your Humpty Dumpties and use the eggs to make a batch of pat-a-cakes.

In a large bowl mix:

5 cups flour

5 teaspoons baking powder

1½ cups sugar

Make a well in the dry ingredients and into it add:

5 eggs

1 cup oil

3 teaspoons vanilla

Mix into a dough.

Give each child a fork. Let each take some dough and roll it into a ball about 2 inches in diameter. Then, as you recite the Pat-a-Cake nursery rhyme aloud (look in a Mother Goose book if you don't know the words), let them pat it flat on the table, prick it with the fork, and then with the fork mark their initials. Repeat as many times as you have dough for everyone.

Carefully remove the pat-a-cakes from the table with a spatula and place on a baking sheet. Bake at 350°F for about 10 minutes. Enjoy!

BE KIND TO ANIMALS WEEK

The American Humane Association has designated the first full week of May as "Be Kind to Animals Week." This is a good time to talk with the children about responsible care of pets.

What do our pets need from us? Food, water, and shelter are easy to think of but love and attention are just as important to their well-being.

After your discussion, enjoy the following activity.

Pet Pictures

You will need:

Paper
Pencil
Crayons or markers

Give each child a sheet of paper, a pencil, and crayons or markers. Let them draw pictures of their pets. Children who do not have a pet can draw a picture of the pet they would like to have.

When the pictures are complete, display them and give each child a chance to tell a little about his or her pet.

Puppy Care and Other Critters, Too! by Judy Petersen Flemming and Bill Flemming, Tambourine Books, 1994.

The fifth of May, *Cinco de Mayo* in Spanish, is a national holiday in Mexico. It commemorates the Mexican victory over the French at the Battle of Puebla, May 5, 1862. This victory was an important step for Mexico in her fight for independence. Today in Mexico and in Mexican-American communities, May 5 brings celebration, fiestas, and parades.

Locate Mexico on a globe or world map. What countries are Mexico's neighbors? Where is Mexico in relation to your location? What route might you travel to get there?

To learn more about Cinco de Mayo see:

 *Fiesta! Cinco de Mayo* by June Behrens, Childrens Press, 1978.

Piñata

You will need:

Balloons of different sizes
Cardboard tubes
Lots of newspaper
5 pounds flour
Masking tape
Colored tissue
Paint (optional)
White craft glue
Scissors
String
Pencil

Piñatas are available in most stores where party supplies are sold. They come in a wide variety of shapes and are quite inexpensive. You may want to purchase one and fill it with goodies for your Cinco de Mayo Mexican fiesta.

Or you can have the fun of making your own piñata. Just be sure to allow at least a week for the piñata to dry before filling it.

1. Decide what shape you are making. Animals are fun but piñatas can be any shape you want.
2. Blow up the balloons. From these and the cardboard tubes you will form the basic shape of the piñata. For example, for a donkey piñata you could use a large balloon for a body, a smaller balloon for a head, and four cardboard tubes for legs. Tape balloons and tubes together to form the basic shape.
3. Next tear the newspaper into long thin strips (about 1 inch wide and at least 12 inches long). You'll need lots of strips.
4. In a large bowl, mix flour and water until it is about the consistency of pancake batter. Dip the newspaper strips in the flour and water mixture, wetting them completely.
5. Remove the excess moisture from the newspaper strips by running them through your fingers. Then drape the newspaper strips over the balloon and cardboard figure. Continue overlapping the strips until the figure is completely covered.
6. Add more and more layers of newspaper until you have applied 5 to 10 layers.
7. To decorate your piñata, let it dry completely. Then you can either paint it or cover it with colored tissue paper attached with white craft glue. Overlap the strips of tissue like shingles.
8. To fill the piñata, cut a small flap in the top, bend it back carefully, and drop in small wrapped candies or novelty items. When the piñata is filled, fold the flap back in place.
9. To hang the piñata, poke a small hole in the top. Tie a string to a pencil, insert the pencil in the hole, and hang by the string.
10. Save your piñata for the Mexican Fiesta.

Serape

You will need:

Large brown paper grocery bag

Scissors

Masking tape

Paint and paintbrushes

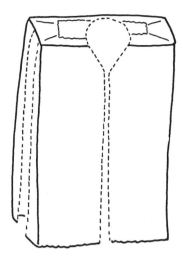

A traditional Mexican serape can be our costume for our Cinco de Mayo festivities. Here is an easy way to make one.

For each child use one brown paper grocery bag. Let each child:

1. Cut straight up the seam on the back of the bag, branching into a "V" and then a hole in the bottom of the bag (this is the neck hole).

2. Next, cut about a 5-inch wide strip from each side of the bag. This makes the open sides of the serape.

3. Cut all around the edges of the two front panels, the back, and the bottom, making a fringe about 1 inch deep all around.

4. Now turn the serape inside out so that the print is inside and the side that is showing is plain brown. You may need to secure the shoulder area (the bottom of the bag) with masking tape.

5. Lay the serapes out flat and paint them with bold designs in bright colors. Make sure you add your name to your serape. Then put them aside to wear for the Mexican fiesta.

Maracas

You will need:

9-inch paper plate

Markers or crayons

Handful of dried beans or rice

Stapler

Five or six 12-inch strips of colored crepe paper

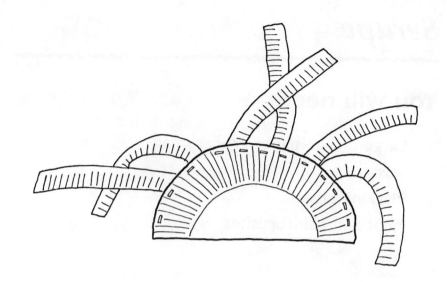

Folk music and dancing are a distinctive part of Mexican culture. You may want to listen to Mexican music during your fiesta. You can join in with the rhythm section with these maracas.

1. Give each child a paper plate. Let them color the plate on the back (convex side) in a bold design with vivid colors.
2. Let each child fold the paper plate in half. Give everyone a handful of dried beans or rice to put in the paper plate. Then staple it shut.
3. Staple 5 or 6 different colored strips of crepe paper about 12 inches long to the curved side of the plate. Your hand holds the folded side.

   Now shake your maraca and make your own music!

Mexican Greetings

Since Spanish is the language of Mexico, help the children learn a few simple Spanish words.

When Mexican children greet each other, they often say *"hola"* (oh´ lah). *Hola* means hello. Practice greeting each other by name the Mexican way!

And when it's time to say goodbye, say *"Adios"* (ah dee ohs´).

At your Cinco de Mayo fiesta, when refreshments are offered, remember your manners the Mexican way with *por favor* (por fah vor´) for please and *gracias* (grah´ see ahs) for thank you!

A Mexican Fiesta

Now put everything together for a Cinco de Mayo Mexican fiesta. Fiesta is the Spanish word for party.

Start with a parade around the building or neighborhood.

Include a tape of traditional Mexican music. Everyone should wear serapes and shake the maracas. Greet your friends the Mexican way.

Before cracking open your piñata and enjoying the sweets inside, try the following two Mexican snacks.

A Taste of Mexico—Nachos

Let the children:

1. Spread tortilla chips evenly on a baking tray.
2. Grate some mild cheddar or Monterey Jack cheese and sprinkle it evenly over the chips.
3. Bake in a 350°F oven just until the cheese is melted—about 5 to 10 minutes.
4. Give each child a small container of salsa to dip their nachos in if they choose.

Nachos and salsa can make you thirsty, so try the following recipe for a nonalcoholic version of a traditional Mexican beverage.

A Taste of Mexico—Sangria

In a large bowl let the children mix:

4 parts purple grape juice

2 parts seltzer

1½ parts orange juice

Help the children slice one or two oranges into thin, round slices. Add these to the sangria. Enjoy!

On this day in 1860, James Matthew Barrie was born in Scotland. Successful as a journalist, novelist, and playwright, most of us remember Barrie as the author of the children's classic *Peter Pan*. Before he died, Barrie bequeathed all of his royalties from *Peter Pan* to the Great Ormond Street Hospital for Sick Children in London. So every time someone buys the book or watches the play or movie about the boy who never grew up, it improves the chances for some other children to get well and grow up!

In honor of Sir James Barrie's birthday, read the children an excerpt from:

📖 **Peter Pan** by J. M. Barrie, Charles Scribner's Sons, 1911.

A Peter Pan Poll

The book *Peter Pan* begins, "All children, except one, grow up." But if it were up to you, would you?

Peter Pan chose to stay a boy forever. The lost boys chose to go back with Wendy, Michael, and John and grow up. Which would you choose?

Conduct a poll on whether the children would choose to stay children forever or grow up.

Tabulate the results on a chart or blackboard but be certain that you also include each child's reasons for his or her choice. Talk about the results.

The following two books offer two children's perspectives of the advantages of being big and little.

📖 **When I Am Big** by Robert Paul Smith, Harper & Row, 1965.

📖 **I Like to Be Little** by Charlotte Zolotow, Harper & Row, 1966.

The pioneer of environmental science, Rachel Carson, was born on May 27, 1907, on a farm in Springdale, Pennsylvania. Carson combined her interest in writing and science when she published the bestselling books *The Sea Around Us*, *Under the Sea Wind*, *The Edge of the Sea*, and her most famous book, *Silent Spring*.

Silent Spring questioned both the chemical companies and the U.S. government for calling the insecticide DDT "safe" when, in fact, it was hazardous to other animals and people as well as the insects on which it was used. As a result of *Silent Spring* the sale and transport of DDT in the United States was stopped in 1973.

The following book is a good juvenile biography of Rachel Carson that includes clear and understandable information on pesticides.

Rachel Carson: Friend of Nature by Carol Greene, Childrens Press, 1992.

Insects—What Good Are They?

Many children think of insects as pests that do nothing but sting or bite people. Some think insects are "creepy" and some are afraid of them.

As Rachel Carson knew, insects are useful to people in many ways. The following song is a fun way for the children to learn to see insects in a more positive light. When you sing, pause after "who are we" in each stanza and give the children a chance to guess the insect.

113

SUNG TO THE TUNE OF "FOUND A PEANUT"

We can fly and we make honey
We can pollinate the trees
And all the pretty flowers.
Who are we? We are the bees.

We can crawl and we dig tunnels
Turning earth beneath your plants,
So your vegetables grow better.
Who are we? We are the ants.

We keep pests out of your garden
With no chemicals or drugs.
We are shiny red with black dots.
Who are we? We're ladybugs.

In the summer, you may see us
Lighting up the evening skies.
We are beautiful to look at.
Who are we? We're fireflies.

So the next time that an insect
Crawls or flutters by your face,
Let him go! He's busy working
Making earth a better place.

Ladybug Bingo

You will need:

Copy of the following illustration
Markers or crayons
Scissors
I die

Even when we appreciate them, there are still times we need to control insects. Just as the insect song says, bringing ladybugs into your garden or farm is an environmentally safe way to keep other insects from eating all the crops.

If you'd like to learn more about the helpful ladybug, see:

The Life Cycle of a Ladybug by Jill Bailey, Bookwright Press, 1989.

When you have finished reading, here is a fun counting game young children will enjoy.

1. Copy the following page and cut it in half so each child gets half a page. This is the bingo card and the squares on the right side are the markers.

2. Let the children color their ladybugs red

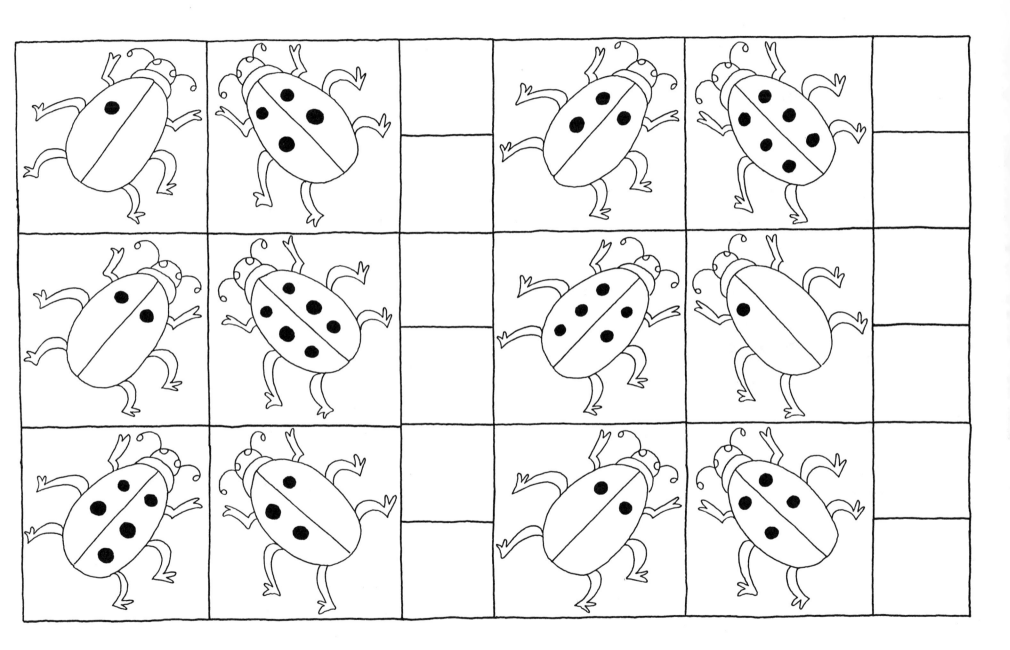

and their markers any colors they want. Then have them cut off the marker strip and cut it into six square markers.

3. Let each child, in turn, roll a die and count the dots on the side facing up. Find the ladybug on the card that has the same number of dots and cover that bug with a marker.

4. If, as the game progresses, a child rolls a number that the children have already covered, he or she must pass the die on and try again next time.

5. The first child to completely cover his or her card shouts "Ladybug Bingo" and wins!

Painted Butterflies

You will need:

Copy of the following illustration
Scissors
Glue
Cardboard
Pencil
One 12-by-18-inch piece of colored paper
Different-colored paint
Eyedropper or spoon
Black crayon or marker

One of the insects that benefited from the ban of DDT is the butterfly.

There are twenty thousand different kinds of butterflies in the world and they come in all the colors of the rainbow and every design imaginable. Butterflies, like many natural creations, are symmetrical. Their two wings have the same design and color.

We can create our own beautiful butterflies with symmetrical wings.

1. Copy the half butterfly shape on the following page. Cut it out, glue it onto cardboard, and cut it out again. The children can trace this pattern to make their butterflies.

2. Let the children choose a 12-by-18-inch piece of paper in any color they like. Fold the paper in half so that it is 9 by 12 inches.

3. Lay the butterfly pattern on top of the paper with the body side along the fold. Trace and cut out.

4. Open the paper flat. Now with an eyedropper or a spoon, drizzle different-colored paint in any pattern you like *on one wing only*. When you are finished applying paint, refold on the fold line, carefully pressing the unpainted wing onto the painted one. Press evenly with your hands.

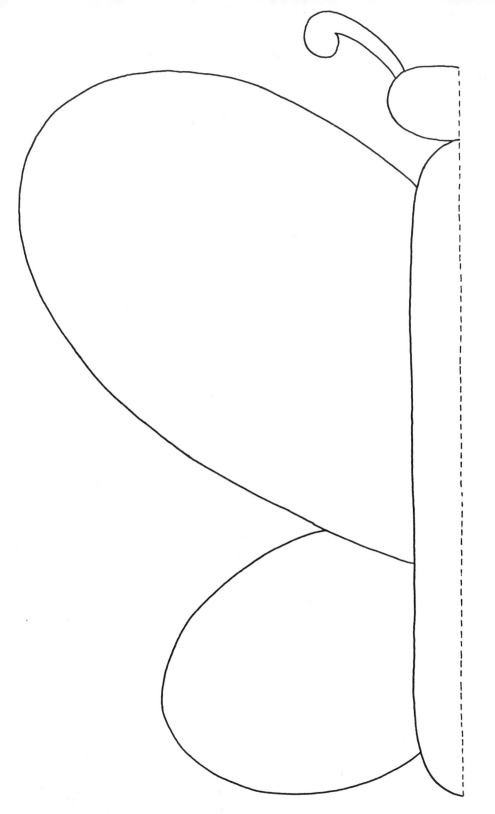

5. Carefully open the butterfly again. You should have the same beautiful design on both wings. Let dry.

6. With crayon or marker, color the body and antennae black. Now display your unique butterflies. Just like real butterflies, no two are exactly alike.

Share these fascinating butterfly facts with the children.

- Butterflies' beautiful wings are covered with overlapping scales (like the shingles on a house or roof). No other insects have scales.

- Butterflies flourish in the tropical rain forest, which is home to more than ten thousand species. As the rain forests are destroyed, thousands of these species have become extinct and many more are endangered.

- Monarch butterflies migrate from North America to Mexico and back (as far as four thousand miles in one year). The trip begun by one generation is completed by the next.

For more fascinating facts on butterflies, read:

Butterflies and Moths by Denny Robson, Gloucester Press, 1986.

Memorial Day was first celebrated shortly after the Civil War. Originally called "Decoration Day," it was a day set aside for decorating the graves of those who had died in military service to our country.

Today, most states in the United States, Washington, D.C., and Puerto Rico have established Memorial Day as a legal holiday at the end of May. Some communities have parades and special ceremonies to honor Americans who have died in wars.

You may enjoy looking at the following book.

Our National Holidays by Karen Spies, Milbrook Press, 1992.

Tissue Poppies

You will need:

Large sheet of red tissue paper
Scissors
One 12-inch pipe cleaner

John McCrae, a Canadian doctor, served in the military in World War I. In 1915, three years before he died, he wrote a poem that begins:

In Flanders fields the poppies blow
Between the crosses, row on row

Since World War I, poppies have become a symbol of Memorial Day. After World War I, veterans first sold artificial poppies to raise funds for French and Belgian war orphans. Today when you give a donation to a veterans' group, you are often given a red poppy to wear to remind you of those who died in service to our country.

Here is a way to make red tissue poppies to wear or use as Memorial Day decorations.

1. Cut a large sheet of red tissue into six rectangles and stack them on top of each other. Cut the paper size according to the size flower you want.
2. Stack all the tissue together and fold the long side of the stack back and forth at about 1/2-inch intervals like an accordion until it is all folded. Hold the "accordion" together by twisting the end of a 12-inch pipe cleaner around the center.
3. Now fold the tissue in half and wrap the pipe cleaner around the folded end several times. The long end of the pipe cleaner is the flower stem.
4. Now carefully stretch apart all the layers of tissue until you have a lovely poppy.

A Happy Memory

〰〰〰〰〰〰〰〰〰〰〰〰〰〰〰〰〰

You will need:

I sheet of drawing paper
Pencil
Crayons or markers

Memorial Day is a bittersweet holiday with pride and gratitude in our veterans mixed with sorrow at the tragic loss war always brings.

Take the time to remind the children that remembering isn't always sad. We all have happy memories and sometimes our happiest ones are not of a big holiday. Let the children try to remember an "everyday" memory of some average day that somehow became special.

- an unexpected visit from someone special
- a special time with a parent, just the two of you
- a special accomplishment—you mastered riding your bike, you painted that great picture, you hit that game-winning home run

1. Give each child a sheet of drawing paper with the words "I REMEMBER" printed across the top. Let older children finish the sentence, describing a special happy memory. For very young children, let them dictate a sentence or phrase describing their happy memory and write it on the paper exactly as they dictate it.
2. Now give the children pencils, crayons, or markers and let them illustrate their happy memory.
3. When everyone is finished, display the pictures and share the memories.

Remind the children that a happy experience is never gone as long as we can remember it.

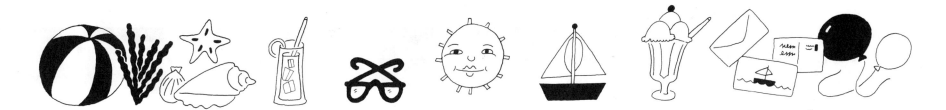

JUNE

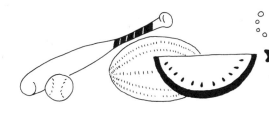

JUNE IS NATIONAL DAIRY MONTH

Since 1937, June has been designated National Dairy Month. The following two activities should help the children appreciate dairy products.

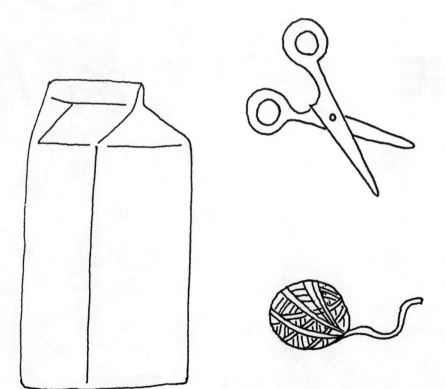

Milk a Cow

You will need:

Copy of the following illustration
Scissors
Glue
Heavy cardboard
Staple gun
Sawhorse
Surgical rubber gloves
Needle
Milk (diluted with water)
Piece of twine or string
Bucket
Low stool or milk crate

Unless you live out in the country, the children in your care probably have never milked a cow. Here is a fun way for city and suburban children to be dairy farmers for a day.

123

1. Make one copy of the cow head and tail on the previous page. Cut them out, glue them onto heavy cardboard, and cut them out again.

2. Using a heavy-duty stapler, attach the head and tail onto opposite ends of a sawhorse.

3. Now take a surgical rubber glove (available at any drugstore) and with a needle, poke a hole at the end of each finger and thumb. Hold the glove open while another person pours milk into it (you can dilute the milk with water), leaving enough room to tie the "wrist" of the glove shut with a long piece of twine. Then tie the full glove to the crosspiece of the sawhorse so that the finger "teats" hang down.

4. Put a pail under your "cow" and a low stool or upturned milk crate next to her. Now give each of the children a turn to milk. Let them squeeze and pull down on the "teats" until the milk squirts into the pail.

   Refill your "cow" until everyone gets a turn.

Milkshakes

Here's a delicious way to enjoy dairy products. Into a blender container pour: $3/4$ cup milk and 1 scoop of your favorite ice cream. Blend until smooth and frothy. Enjoy! This recipe will serve 1 to 2 children.

The great American architect, Frank Lloyd Wright, was born on June 8, 1867. Making use of the latest technology, Wright created buildings that were inspired by nature and designed to harmonize with their natural surroundings. Some of his more famous buildings include the Solomon R. Guggenheim Museum in New York City, the Imperial Hotel in Tokyo, and the Kaufmann House (Fallingwater) in Bear Run, Pennsylvania.

Architect for a Day

You will need:

Photographs and books on the work of Frank Lloyd Wright

Blueprints

Pencil with eraser

Ruler

Scrap paper

Graph paper

Check your library under call number 720 and get some materials on architecture in general and Frank Lloyd Wright in particular.

Show the children photographs of some of Wright's buildings as well as architectural plans or blueprints.

1. Talk with the children about the work of an architect. Do they realize that before any building is built, it is drawn on paper? Look closely at the blueprints and notice what the symbols represent. Talk about drawing to scale and what the scale is on the drawings you are looking at.

2. Now it is the children's turn to be architects. Give each child a pencil, an eraser, a ruler, some scrap paper, and some graph paper. (Older children can draw to scale and younger children will enjoy using the special paper even if they don't draw to scale.) Their commission is to design their own playhouses.

3. Before putting any lines on the paper, the children should be encouraged to stop and think. An architect designs a building according to how it will be used. Ask the children:

- What do you want in your playhouse?
- What kinds of space do you need?
- What will you be playing there?

    Remind them that the sky is the limit on size, shape, windows, doors, floors, etc.

4. Now let them design their ideal playhouses first on scrap paper. When they have worked out the details, they can transfer the design to graph paper. Then they can draw in all the furnishings.

5. When the drawing is done, display all the floor plans. Let each "architect" review his or her design for the group.

You can learn more about Frank Lloyd Wright and enjoy many other activities that are related to his life and ideas by reading:

Frank Lloyd Wright for Kids by Kathleen Thorne-Thomsen, Chicago Review Press, 1994.

      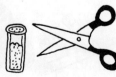 

In Brooklyn, New York, on June 10, 1928, the wonderful artist and illustrator Maurice Sendak was born. Sendak has illustrated ninety children's books but is probably most famous for two picture books he both wrote and illustrated, *Where the Wild Things Are* (the Caldecott Medal Winner for 1964) and *In the Night Kitchen.*

In honor of Sendak's birthday, read aloud to the children:

Where the Wild Things Are by Maurice Sendak, Harper, 1963.

Talk to the children about the fact that a long, long time ago, before there were any people, our planet was inhabited by many wonderful "wild things" called dinosaurs.

Be certain young children understand that although there are no dinosaurs today, they are not make-believe like Sendak's "wild things." They really lived but are now extinct.

There are many, many great books about dinosaurs. Check your library under call number J567.9 and borrow several for the children to browse through.

Here is one young children will probably enjoy:

A New True Book: Dinosaurs by Mary Lou Clark, Childrens Press, 1981.

Older children should like:

Dinosaur & Other Prehistoric Fact Finder by Dr. Michael Benton, Kingfisher Books, 1992.

Make Your Own Prehistoric Wild Things

Now that you have seen pictures of what paleontologists believe dinosaurs looked like, make some yourselves out of clay.

Here is a recipe for clay the children can make themselves.

Ingredients

3 cups flour
1 cup salt
1 cup water
1/2 cup vegetable oil

Mix flour and salt together. Gradually add water and oil and knead into a dough.

The dough will keep in a covered jar in the refrigerator. If you leave your sculptures out in the air, they will harden.

Remember, dinosaurs came in many shapes and sizes. In fact, no one knows for certain what all the dinosaurs looked like so the children can either try to replicate dinosaurs from the pictures they have seen or they can create their own.

When the dinosaur sculptures are dry, they can be painted.

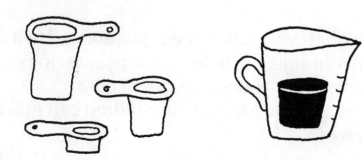

Build a World for Your Wild Things

You will need:

Cardboard box
Paint and markers
Old magazines

The dinosaur sculptures need a place to live.

1. Take a rectangular cardboard box and turn it so that the open end faces you. The inside top and bottom are the sky and ground. Paint the sky and decorate the ground according to the kind of environment you want for your dinosaurs: ocean, beach, desert, marsh, forest, etc.

2. Now decorate the sides with paint or cut out pictures to represent the dinosaurs' world. Are there trees, waves, mountains, volcanoes, sand dunes? You decide.

3. When the box is dry, set your clay dinosaurs in it.

Recyclesaurus—A Group Project

You will need:

Any good "junk" (boxes, milk or egg cartons,
   cardboard tubes, etc.)
Tape or glue
Paint

Here's a "wild thing" everyone can make together.

Using cardboard boxes, clean empty milk cartons, cardboard tubes, and any other good "junk" you can find, build your own creature. Tape or glue the parts together.

Egg cartons make great scales. Two closed egg cartons attached at one end make a great mouth. The egg carton cups look like teeth. Egg cups cut off the carton and painted make good bulging eyes. Cardboard tubes make terrific spikes, and milk cartons work well for legs.

Either paint the parts separately or wait until the creature is assembled. Be creative! No one knows exactly what color dinosaurs were.

Dinosaurs' names describe them. Since this one is made from all previously used materials, you can call him "Recyclesaurus"!

Before leaving the dinosaurs, here's a wonderful story to enjoy with the children.

Dinosaur Bob & His Adventures with the Family Lazardo by William Joyce, Harper & Row, 1988.

On June 14, 1777, the American flag of thirteen stars and thirteen stripes was approved by the new American government. On the same day in 1916, President Woodrow Wilson proclaimed Flag Day to be a national holiday celebrated every June 14.

Do the children know that on today's flag the fifty stars represent the fifty states?

A good book to read in honor of the day is:

Our National Holidays by Karen Spies, Millbrook Press, 1992.

Design Your Own Flag

You will need:

1 sheet of colored drawing paper
Markers or crayons
Old magazines or catalogs
Glue

Talk to the children about a flag as a symbol. In the American flag, for example, everything means something. The fifty stars represent the fifty states, while the thirteen stripes stand for the thirteen colonies with which America started. Even the colors are significant: red symbolizes courage, white is for purity, and blue stands for perseverance and justice.

Let each child design a personal flag to represent him- or herself.

Tell the children:

1. Your first decision is the choice of color for the background—your favorite color or a color that is symbolic of you. For example, if you love the outdoors, green may be appropriate. A "night person" may choose purple, black, or dark blue for a background.

   Give each child a sheet of paper in the color of his or her choice.

2. For the symbols on the flag, take some time to think about yourself.

   Do you have any hobbies? If you are an artist, a paintbrush or palette might be on your flag. If you are an athlete, you might have a tennis racquet or soccer ball, etc. If you like to read, books. If you are a musician, your instrument. Anything that describes you is an appropriate symbol.

   Include as many different symbols as it takes to describe your whole personality. Draw them on your flag or cut them out and paste them on.

3. Display all the flags around the room. Looking at them should tell you a lot about the individuals in your group.

Ancestral Flags

You will need:

One 12-by-18-inch sheet of white drawing paper
Pencil
Reference book with flags from all countries
Crayons or markers

Here in America, we have always been a melting pot. Americans come from all over the world. Now that the world is our children's neighborhood, it is even more interesting for them to investigate their heritage.

     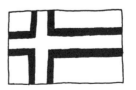 

Before you begin this project the children have some homework to do. They need to find out what countries their ancestors came from in both their father's and mother's families. If any children in your group were adopted from other countries, their ancestry would be their biological background if that is available.

1. Give each child a 12-by-18-inch sheet of white drawing paper. Let the children draw a line dividing the paper into two 9-by-12-inch rectangles. One rectangle is for their ancestry on their mother's side and the other for their father's.

2. Bring out reference materials with pictures of flags from around the world. Most encyclopedias have colored illustrations of international flags under "F." Also check your library under nonfiction call number J929.9 for books on flags of the world. Be sure to have several books available since all the children will be referring to them.

3. Let the children copy their ancestral flags using pencil, crayons, or markers. Complicated flags don't have to be perfect, just recognizable. Each child will have at least two flags on his/her ancestral flag. (They could be two of the same flag.) However, some children could have many more than two. For example, if your mother's family is Italian and your father's is a combination of English, Irish, and German, your flag will have a large Italian flag filling one-half of the paper, and three flags (of England, Ireland, and Germany) filling the other half.

4. When the flags are finished, display them and see how far you all have come to get here!

In the Northern Hemisphere, the summer solstice is the longest day (and the shortest night) of the year and begins the summer season. If June 22 brings summer in your neighborhood, try the next two activities.

"Wish I Were Here" Postcards

You will need:

One 5-by-7-inch piece of white posterboard
Pencils, crayons, or markers
Black adhesive photo corners
Black pen

For many of us, summer is vacation time. Talk with the children about their ideas for the perfect vacation trip. Where would they go? How would they get there? What would they do there? How long would they stay?

After you've talked for a while, let the children make postcards of their ideal vacation.

1. Give each child a 5-by-7-inch piece of white posterboard on which you've drawn a ½-inch margin all around.

2. Using pencils, crayons, or markers, let each child draw a colorful picture illustrating the perfect vacation. Keep all drawings inside the margin.

3. When the pictures are finished, let or help the children write the name of the chosen vacation spot in black ink on the bottom white margin. (If someone's idea of the perfect vacation is relaxing in her own pool, "My Backyard Pool" is a perfect caption.)

4. Prepare a bulletin board entitled "Wish We Were Here!" Using black adhesive photo corners, mount the "postcards" on the bulletin board.

   It should be fun to see all the different possibilities for a perfect vacation.

Watermelon Craft

You will need:

I piece of watermelon with seeds

I sheet of green construction paper

I sheet of white construction paper

I sheet of red construction paper

Pencils

Scissors

Glue

Start this activity with a refreshing snack of fresh watermelon and save the seeds. Lay them on a paper to dry.

The following craft should be worked on in pairs.

1. Give each pair of children three sheets of construction paper, one green, one white, and one red, plus pencils, scissors, and glue.

2. Have one child trace the largest possible circle that will fit on the green paper (use a compass, or trace a circular object) and cut it out. Fold it in half, open it, and cut on the fold line. Give one green half circle to the partner.

3. Meanwhile, the second child traces a circle on the white paper $1/2$ to 1 inch smaller in diameter than the green circle. Cut it out, fold it in half, open it, and cut on the fold line. Give one white half circle to the partner.

4. Whoever finishes first should trace a circle on the red paper $1/2$ to 1 inch smaller in diameter than the white circle. Cut it out. Fold it in half, open it, and cut on the fold line. Give one red half circle to the partner.

5. Now both children stack the half circles with the "smallest" (red) on top, then white, then green, with the straight edges lined up. (On the curved edge you have an arc of green, then one of white, then a red half circle.) Glue the white to the green, then the red on top. You have a piece of seedless watermelon!

6. Now add the final touch and glue on real watermelon seeds. You have a slice of summer!

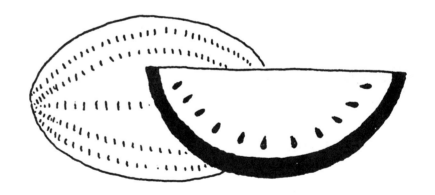

Today is the birthday of Olympic track star Wilma Rudolph. As a child Rudolph was partially paralyzed by polio and wore a leg brace until she was twelve years old. At age twenty, in the 1960 Olympic Games, Wilma Rudolph became the first American woman runner to receive three gold medals.

One of the events Wilma Rudolph won a gold medal for was the relay race. Celebrate the birthday of this inspiring athlete by holding your own.

Rudolph Relays

You will need:

At least 4 children
1 "baton" per team
Area to race

1. Depending on the number of children in your group, divide them into teams of 2, 3, or 4 each.

2. Establish a starting line and finish line. Depending on how many children are on each team, divide up the distance of the course equally and position team members at the starting line and at the start of each segment.

3. Give the starter on each team a "baton." A long cardboard tube is fine.

4. When everyone is in position shout, "On your mark, get set, GO!" The starting runner on each team runs to the second member of the team and passes the baton. The second runner continues, etc., until the baton is passed to the final runner. The first team to have a runner cross the finish line wins the gold!

It should be no surprise that Mildrid "Babe" Didrikson Zaharias, born on this day in 1914, was named woman athlete of the first half of the twentieth century. Zaharias excelled in golf, track and field, basketball, baseball, swimming, diving, and billiards. Winner of two gold and one silver Olympic medals in 1932, Zaharias has been an inspiration to all athletes, and women athletes in particular, ever since.

A young people's biography with many photographs of this great athlete is:

Babe Didrikson Zaharias by Elizabeth A. Lynn, Chelsea House, 1989.

Practice Putting

Between 1940 and 1950 Babe Didrikson Zaharias won every women's title in golf at least once! Let the children celebrate Babe Zaharias's birthday with a little putting practice.

You will need:

Golf clubs
Golf balls (plastic practice balls are best)
Area for putting
Cup (for older children) or circular target
  on the floor

1. Each child can take a turn putting a few golf balls.
2. Older children can try to putt the ball into a cup. Younger ones can just aim for a circle marked on the floor. (Draw a circle with chalk or cut one out of paper.)

    Did the children find it harder than they thought to hit the ball? Remind them—easy does it!

JUNE 27 | Helen Keller's Birthday

Helen Keller was born on June 27, 1880 on a farm in Alabama. When she was just eighteen months old she had a serious illness that left her deaf and blind. Since she could not hear, Helen did not learn to speak as a young child. She had no effective way of communicating until a dedicated teacher, Anne Sullivan, came into her life.

In the years that followed, working with her teacher, Helen learned so much that she eventually graduated college with honors and published several books. Helen Keller has become an inspiration to physically challenged people everywhere.

To learn more about the life of this fascinating woman, read:

Helen Keller by Richard Tames, Franklin Watts, 1989.

"Sign" Your Name

One of the ways Anne Sullivan taught Helen Keller to communicate was by fingerspelling, using a manual alphabet.

The following book beautifully illustrates the manual alphabet.

The Handmade Alphabet by Laura Rankin, Dial Books, 1991.

Copy the chart of the manual alphabet on the following page, making one copy for each child.

Let the children work together figuring out how to fingerspell their names.

Why do the children think sign language, which uses hand signs to represent entire words, is used more often than the manual alphabet?

Helen Keller's birthday is a good time to do some activities on our five senses, especially with young children.

139

As a baby, Helen Keller lost the use of two of her five senses. Often we take our five senses for granted. We don't realize how much we use our seeing, hearing, tasting, touching, and smelling to learn about the world around us. The following six activities can help the children become more aware of how much we count on our five senses.

Sight—I Spy

This is an enjoyable way to get children to use their powers of observation.

You start the game by saying, "I spy, with my two eyes something _____." Fill in the blank with a one-word description of an object in sight. Describe the object's color, size, shape, etc.

Let the children keep looking around and guessing until someone guesses what you spied. Then that person can take a turn giving a clue about a new object.

When you have finished playing, settle down for a talk. Explain to the children that while most of us "see" with our eyes, blind people have their own special way of "seeing." The following book explains the concept beautifully.

Through Grandpa's Eyes by Patricia MacLachlan, Harper & Row, 1980.

Hearing—Whispering down the Lane

This game is fun for children of any age.

Let the children sit or stand in a circle. Let one person in line whisper a sentence into the ear of the person next to him. He must whisper very softly and say the sentence only once. The second person then softly whispers whatever she thinks she heard to the person next to her, and so on until everyone has had a turn.

The last person says whatever he heard aloud to the group. Is it the same message the first person whispered? Sometimes our sense of hearing can play tricks on us!

Explain to the children that for hearing-impaired people, normal conversations may be as difficult to hear as our "whispering down the lane." Some people cannot hear even the loudest sounds.

The following book can give the children some insight into what it is like to be deaf.

I Have A Sister, My Sister Is Deaf by Jeanne Whitehouse Peterson, Harper & Row, 1977.

Taste Test

You will need:

Several samples of sweet, sour, salty, and bitter
   foods for the children to taste

We taste through our taste buds located on our tongues. Although it may seem that we have tasted thousands of different flavors, we really can only distinguish four different tastes: sweet, sour, salty, and bitter.

First, give the children a sample of each of these "tastes" to taste:

A spoonful of sugar (sweet)

A piece of lemon (sour)

A potato chip (salty)

Some cocoa powder (bitter)—*not* hot
   chocolate mix

Now that they have the idea of what sweet, sour, salty, and bitter taste like, provide a selection of foods for them to taste and try to classify in one of the four taste categories.

Here are some foods you may want to include:

Honey, pancake syrup, raisins, brown sugar, marshmallows, jam.

Pickles (sweet and dill), grapefruit, sourball candy.

Salted nuts, green olives, bacon bits, pretzels, peanut butter.

Coffee (beans, ground, or crystals), endive, ground cinnamon.

Finally, sometimes our sense of smell can deceive us about how something will taste. Let the children smell an open bottle of vanilla extract. Then let them taste a little on their fingertip. Does it taste the way they thought it would?

Touch—A Cooperative Collage of Textures

You will need:

Sheets of computer paper

Tape

Glue

Textured "scraps" (rough, smooth, soft, and hard)

1. Cover a large area of the floor with computer paper taped together. Be sure there is enough paper so all the children in the group can work together comfortably.

2. Now provide glue and lots of different textured scraps. The children are going to glue the scrap materials onto the paper, overlapping them until the paper is completely covered. Here are some ideas for the scraps.

   Rough-textured items: sandpaper of varying coarseness, burlap, textured vinyl floor tile, bark, rope or rough twine, muslin, rough wood, cork.

   Smooth-textured items: satin, scraps of ribbon, plastic pages from photo albums.

   Soft-textured items: velvet, carpet scraps, fake fur, cotton balls.

   Hard items: stones, rocks, shells, marbles, smooth wood.

   Any item you have available can become a part of the texture collage.

3. When the glue is dry, hang up the collage. Then let the children close their eyes and "look" at their collage with their fingers. This tactile experience has been brought to you by your sense of touch.

142

Smell—Cupcake Flowers

You will need:

1 sheet of drawing paper

Crayons

A few different colored cupcake baking cups

Glue

2 or 3 different scents of cologne

1. Give each child a sheet of drawing paper and some crayons. Let them color in some grass and some flower stems and leaves. They should not draw the blossom part of the flower.
2. Next, give each child a few different colored paper cupcake baking cups. These are their flower blossoms. Have them glue the cupcake cups to the stems.
3. The final touch is to add the scent to the flowers. Provide the children with two or three different scents of cologne. (Spray bottles work best.) Let them add just one drop or one spray of cologne to the blossoms of their flowers.

   Remind them it is our sense of smell that lets us enjoy these fragrant flowers.

Five Senses Snack

Here's a nutritious snack that we can enjoy with all five of our senses—popcorn!

First pass around the unpopped popcorn kernels. Have the children look at their shiny golden color and feel how smooth they are.

Now pop the corn in either a covered pot or a popcorn popper. Listen! You can hear your snack happening!

Sniff! You can smell the aroma of freshly popped corn!

When the popcorn is ready, take a good look at it again. It has changed color and shape. Touch it. The texture is completely different from the unpopped kernels. Feel how light it is now!

Finally, taste and enjoy a delicious treat!

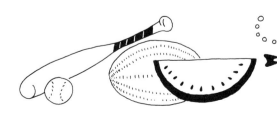

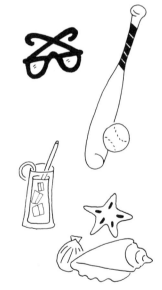

JULY

First locate Canada on a globe or world map. What countries are Canada's neighbors? Where is Canada located in relation to your location? What route might you travel to get there?

July 1 is Canada's birthday. It is a national holiday celebrating the day Canada became an independent nation in 1867. Canada was first a Dominion of England so her independence day was called Dominion Day. Today many Canadians call July 1, Canada Day.

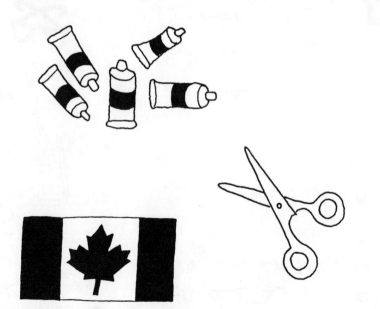

Maple Leaf Art

You will need:

Picture of the flag of Canada
Copy of the following illustration
Scissors
One 9-by-12-inch sheet of art paper—any color
Tempera paint—contrasting color
Toothbrush
Newspaper
Smock

Show the children a picture of the flag of Canada. Explain that the leaf on the flag is a maple leaf. The maple leaf has become a symbol of Canada.

red maple

silver maple

sugar maple

147

1. If you have a maple tree available, show the children a real maple leaf. Then, since we don't want to pick a lot of leaves, make a copy of the previous page for each child in the group. Have the children cut out all the different-sized maple leaf shapes.

2. Let each child choose a sheet of 9-by-12-inch art paper and some tempera paint in a contrasting color (either light paper and dark paint or dark paper and light paint). Pour the paint into a shallow container and give every child a toothbrush.

3. This part is very messy but lots of fun. Cover the work areas with newspaper and be sure everyone wears a smock. Have the children lay their paper maple leaves on top of the art paper, arranging them any way they want—overlapping is fine.

   Now tell them to dip the toothbrushes into the paint. Using the hand that isn't holding the toothbrush, run one finger over the paint-covered bristles, spattering paint onto the art paper. Keep refueling the toothbrush and spattering the paint until all the art paper that isn't covered by leaves is paint-spattered. It doesn't matter if the leaves are painted. Concentrate on the 9-by-12-inch paper.

4. Now carefully remove the paper leaves and see the design you've made. When the paint is dry, you can display your maple leaf designs. Hopefully they will remind the children of our North American neighbor, Canada.

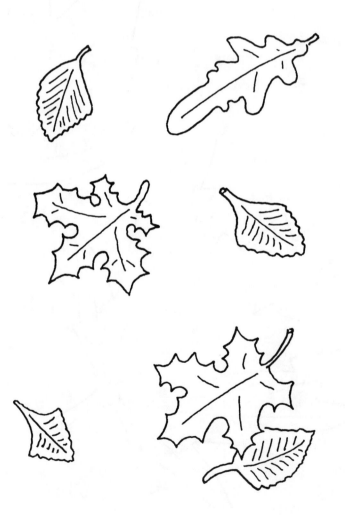

JULY 4 | George M. Cohan's Birthday

George Michael Cohan was born on July 4, 1878 in Providence, Rhode Island. An actor since he was a child, Cohan grew up to succeed as an actor, a playwright, a producer, and a songwriter. Some of his most popular songs were the patriotic ones, including "You're a Grand Old Flag," "Give My Regards to Broadway," "Over There," and "The Yankee Doodle Boy."

A Yankee Doodle Sing-Along

Celebrate the birthday of Mr. Cohan with a sing-along of two of his lively patriotic songs: "You're a Grand Old Flag," created in 1906, and "Yankee Doodle Dandy," created in 1908. Give the children a copy of the lyrics and practice singing with them. Learn the songs well because you will have a chance to sing them again in the Fourth of July Patriotic Parade activity.

YOU'RE A GRAND OLD FLAG

You're a Grand Old Flag
You're a high-flying flag,
And forever in peace may you wave.
You're the emblem of the land I love,
The home of the free and the brave.
Ev'ry heart beats true
'neath the Red White & Blue
Where there's never a boast or brag,
But should auld acquaintance be forgot,
Keep your eye on the grand old flag.

YANKEE DOODLE DANDY

I'm a Yankee Doodle Dandy,
A Yankee Doodle do or die;
A real live nephew of my Uncle Sam
Born on the Fourth of July.
I've got a Yankee Doodle sweetheart,
She's my Yankee Doodle joy.
Yankee Doodle came to London
Just to ride the ponies;
I am the Yankee Doodle Boy.

This is really just the chorus of the song, "The Yankee Doodle Boy." It has come to be sung as a song in its own right.

149

Independence Day is the day we celebrate the birthday of the United States of America.

On July 4, 1776, America announced to the world that she was a free country and no longer a colony of England. Every year since, on the Fourth of July, Americans celebrate their freedom with the flying of flags, parades, festivals, and fireworks. The following three activities are ways you can join in America's birthday party.

A Patriotic Parade

You will need:

Red, white, and blue crepe paper streamers

Red, white, and blue balloons

Large posterboard

Markers or crayons

Have a Fourth of July parade around your building or neighborhood.

If the children have riding toys, decorate them with red, white, and blue crepe paper streamers and red, white, and blue balloons. The children can make and then carry a big posterboard banner that says "Happy Birthday, America" (in red, white, and blue, of course!). Other children can wave American flags.

And every parade needs some rousing music— sing loudly the songs that you just learned, "Yankee Doodle Dandy" and "Grand Old Flag."

Fireworks Art

You will need:

Newspaper
Sheet of black construction paper
White craft glue
Red, silver, and blue glitter

Since fireworks are a traditional part of Independence Day—USA, here is an art project appropriate for the day.

1. Cover the work area with newspaper. Give each child a sheet of black construction paper and a bottle of white craft glue.
2. Let the children draw with the glue, arcing lines from a central dot of glue, in starburst fireworks shapes.
3. Then bring out red, silver, and blue glitter. Let the children cover their glue lines with glitter, making some red, some silver, and some blue fireworks in their black night skies.
4. Keep the artwork flat until it dries. Then display the your fireworks art for everyone to enjoy.

Red, White, and Blueberries

Here is a delicious, nutritious, and patriotic snack for America's Happy Birthday party.

Ingredients

Strawberries and blueberries (enough so that combined they will serve your group)
Whipped cream in an aerosol can

1. Let the children wash the strawberries, hull them and cut them, if necessary, into bite-sized pieces.
2. Let the children wash the blueberries and remove any stems.
3. Next have the children mix the berries in a large bowl and spoon them into individual serving dishes.
4. Finally, each of the children can top the berries with a squirt of whipped cream. Make sure they hold the can straight upside down. As they squirt, you can count "one, two, three." At three they stop squirting so everyone gets an equal share of the cream.

The creator of "The Greatest Show on Earth," Phineas Taylor Barnum was born on July 5, 1810, in Connecticut. A showman all his life, in 1881 Barnum combined his show with the circus of James Anthony Bailey to form the Barnum and Bailey Circus, which has thrilled children around the world ever since.

What better way to celebrate the birthday of P. T. Barnum than with your own circus! The activities that follow will give you some ideas.

Be a Clown

You will need:

Solid, white vegetable shortening
Cornstarch
Food coloring
Dress-up items

No circus would be complete without clowns, so here is a recipe for some homemade face paint.

Mix 1 part vegetable shortening and 2 parts cornstarch in a bowl until thoroughly blended.

This works as is for white face paint. Add food coloring as desired for colored face paint.

Children can enjoy painting their own faces or each other's. They can add round cheeks, colored noses and chins, hearts, rainbows, geometric shapes, etc.

Once their clown faces are on, the rest of the costumes are easy. Big shirts (paint smocks), two different shoes, funny hats, gloves, anything in your dress-up box put together in unusual combinations can be funny.

For their clown acts, the children can try miming, juggling, telling jokes, or doing stunts with jump ropes, hula hoops, riding toys, balloons, water squirt bottles or water balloons, even stilts (see the following activity).

When the children are finished clowning around, wipe the face paint off with tissue, then wash well with soap and water.

Circus Stilts

You will need:

2 empty coffee cans with plastic lids
  (1 pound size)

Hammer

Awl

Heavy twine

Duct tape

You can make your own circus stilts with empty coffee cans, a hammer and an awl, some heavy twine, and duct tape (both twine and duct tape are available at hardware stores).

1. Turn the cans over so that the open end rests on the floor. With a hammer and an awl poke two holes on the bottom of each can, opposite each other and near the rim of the can.

2. Help each child measure two pieces of twine long enough so that the child can hold the two ends of the twine at chest height while the middle of the twine is under the child's foot.

3. After you've measured and cut the twine, have the children carefully thread the twine through the holes so that the middle of the twine goes across the inside bottom of the can and the two long ends come out the outside of the bottom of the can.

4. Let each child make a line with marker on the spots where the twine comes out of the holes. Pull the twine out from the inside of the can just enough so you can wrap duct tape over those two places on the twine. (Since the twine rubs the cut metal of the can at these two points, the duct tape is necessary to prevent it from fraying and

153

breaking.) To protect the floor, at this point you can cover the open ends of the cans with their plastic lids.

5. Now, with the plastic lids of the cans on the floor, help the children step up on their stilts. The key to walking on them is to wrap the twine around your hands and hold it taut at all times. Pull up on the twine as you step and be careful! How does the world look from up there?

Tightrope Walking

You will need:

Plank or length of clothesline
Umbrella

This is an exercise in balance masquerading as a circus act.

1. Lay a "tightrope" on the ground. This can be a plank or even a length of clothesline pulled straight on the ground.
2. Give each child a brightly colored umbrella to hold in one hand. He or she can hold the other arm straight out to the side. Let the children put one foot in front of the other and carefully walk the tightrope without falling "off."

   Was it harder than they thought or easier?

For children who have a hard time balancing, one tip is for them to pick a spot in front of them at eye level and focus on that spot as they walk.

JULY 7 Tanabata Star Festival—Japan

First locate Japan on a globe or world map. What countries are Japan's neighbors? Where is Japan in relation to your location? What route might you travel to get there?

Tanabata is a festival based on an ancient Chinese love story. Two stars, one a princess, the other a cowherd, fell in love and married. They were so much in love, they neglected their duties. The king of the heavens became angry and sent them to live on opposite sides of the Milky Way. Only once a year, on the seventh day of the seventh month can the two lovers meet.

On this day, the Japanese celebrate by decorating bamboo poles with paper streamers and poems and placing them outside their houses and in their gardens.

Japanese Haiku

You will need:

One 5-by-7-inch piece of colored paper
Bare branches
Bucket with sand or stones
Hole punch
Gift tie

Since Tanabata is a Japanese holiday, we will decorate our branches with traditional Japanese poems, or haiku.

Haiku poems always have three lines. The first and third lines have five syllables. The second line has seven. The lines do not rhyme.

Some wonderful examples of haiku can be found in the following book.

📖 **Red Dragonfly on My Shoulder** translated by Aylvia Cassedy and Kunihiro Suetake, HarperCollins, 1992.

After sharing some haiku with the children, let them try writing some. On a blackboard or chart write the following notes to help the children understand haiku.

HAIKU ARE POEMS ABOUT NATURE

Brainstorm together about the possibilities in nature about which you can write.

HAIKU PAINTS A PICTURE IN WORDS

Haiku has very few words in it, so you must be careful to pick the perfect ones to best describe what you mean.

HAIKU ARE ALWAYS ABOUT RIGHT NOW

These are not poems about what has been or what will be. They are always about the present moment.

HAIKU IS WRITTEN IN THREE SHORT LINES. THE FIRST LINE HAS FIVE SYLLABLES, THE SECOND, SEVEN, AND THE THIRD, FIVE.

Older children can try for the 5-7-5 form but young children may find it too difficult. They can just write three short lines.

HAIKU DOES NOT RHYME

When the children are happy with a haiku they have written, give them different-colored sheets of paper (one each) about 5 by 7 inches and let them print their haiku on the colored paper as beautifully as they can.

You can display the haiku on bare branches supported in a pail of sand or stones (see the Mitten Tree activity). Let each child punch a hole in one end of their haiku paper, thread curling gift tie in it, and tie the paper to a branch.

In celebrating Tanabata, the children may have learned that it can be quite a challenge expressing yourself in very few words!

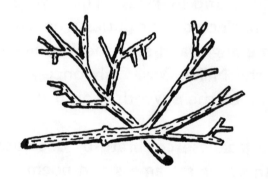

Constellation Star-Gazers

You will need:

Copy of the following illustration
Tube from bathroom tissue
One 4-by-4-inch piece of black paper
1 sheet of tracing paper
Pencil
Hat pin or straight pin
Rubber band
Piece of corrugated cardboard or cork

Since Tanabata is a star festival, star-gazing should certainly be part of the celebration. Here's a way for the children to see some constellations anytime, anywhere!

1. Make a copy of the constellation chart on the next page for each child.
2. Give each child a cardboard tube from bathroom tissue, a 4-by-4-inch piece of black paper, a sheet of tracing paper, a pencil, a hat pin or straight pin, a rubber band, and either a piece of corrugated cardboard (about 4 by 4 inches) or a straw or cork trivet (to work on).
3. Let the children look at all the constellation diagrams and decide which one they want to "view." Have them trace that constellation on tracing paper by just making pencil dots for the stars in the constellation.
4. Now turn the tracing paper over so you are looking at a reverse image of the constellation. Lay the tracing paper on top of the black paper and lay them both on top of the cardboard (or straw or cork).
5. With the pin, prick holes through the tracing paper where the "stars" are. For larger star holes, after you've stuck in the pin, rotate it at an angle and it will tear a bigger round hole.
6. Now discard the tracing paper and put the black paper over one end of the cardboard tube. Center the constellation over the end of the tube and fold the excess paper down over the sides of the tube, securing it with the rubber band.
7. Look through the tube with one eye while facing a light or window. Can you see your constellation shining in the night sky?

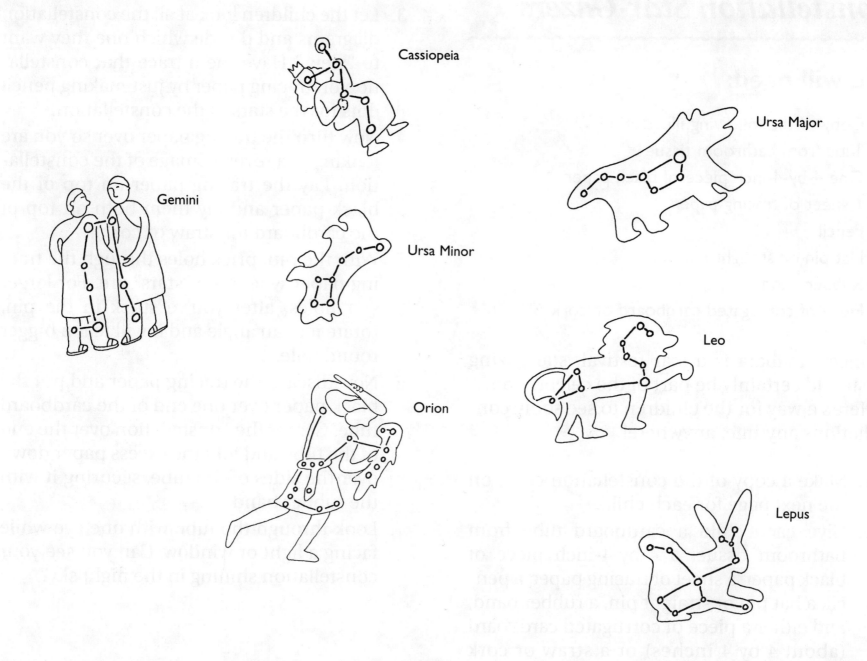

Cassiopeia

Ursa Major

Gemini

Ursa Minor

Leo

Orion

Lepus

158

S p a c e   W e e k

On July 20, 1969 two U.S. astronauts, Neil Armstrong and Edwin Aldrin Jr., became the first two people to set foot on the moon. In some communities the week including July 20 has been designated "Space Week" in honor of this momentous anniversary.

To commemorate Space Week we have a number of celestial activities for you to enjoy.

Before you begin you may want to learn more about astronomy with the following book.

A New True Book: Moon, Sun and Stars by John Lewellen, Childrens Press, 1981.

Lunar Art

You will need:

Pictures of the surface of the moon
1 sheet of black construction paper
Pencil
Scissors
White powdered tempera paint
Liquid starch
White flour
Shallow container for paint
Damp sponge

Celebrate Moon Day on July 20 by creating your own moons complete with cratered surfaces.

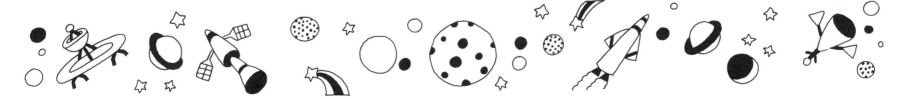

1. Show the children photographs of the surface of the moon and point out its rough, cratered surface.

2. Give each of the children a sheet of black construction paper. Have them each trace a circle on the paper and cut it out.

3. Now work together to mix a batch of "crater paint."

   Mix:

   3 parts white powdered tempera paint

   3 parts liquid starch

   2 parts white flour

      Blend well. The paint will be a thick, sticky paste.

4. Give each child a shallow container of crater paint and a damp sponge. Dip the sponge into the paint, wipe off the excess on the edge of the container, and dab the paint onto the black circles. As you dab the paint on and pull the sponge up, the paint pulls up into a rough texture. (Don't rub the sponge from side to side on the paper.) Continue dabbing on crater paint until the "moon" is mostly white. Some black paper will show through giving the moon a three-dimensional look.

5. Lay the artwork flat to dry. Then be sure the children feel the rough surfaces of the paint. You can display your lunar art in honor of Space Week.

Sun Prints

You will need:

Light-sensitive paper

Small items (paper clips, keys, etc.)

Piece of heavy cardboard or a cookie sheet

Piece of glass or plastic

On a bright sunny day, put solar power to work in creating unique works of art.

To do this activity you need light-sensitive print paper, which is available in many toy stores or scientific hobby stores.

1. Go outside with the light-sensitive paper (covered until you are ready to print) and a collection of small items such as paper clips, buttons, keys, etc. Outside, the children can look for small natural objects such as pebbles, fallen leaves or feathers, small twigs, etc.

2. Give each child a sheet of light-sensitive paper and have him lay it flat on a sheet of heavy cardboard or a cookie sheet. On top of each paper each child can lay an arrangement of any items he chooses. If the children use light-weight objects such as leaves,

feathers, etc., their arrangements should be covered with a sheet of glass or clear plastic. (Borrow some from a picture frame.)

3. Leave the items on the paper for about five minutes (or according to the directions on the print paper).

4. Come back inside to develop the prints following the directions on the print paper package.

These unique prints were created by you in cooperation with the Sun, our nearest star! Display them proudly for Space Week.

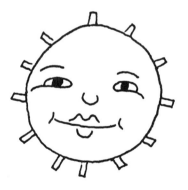

Hands-on Planet Fun

You will need:

Name labels

1 marble

2 golf balls

1 large "shooter" marble

Beach ball—15 to 16 inches in diameter

Beach ball—13 inches in diameter

2 cantaloupes or rubber balls—5 to 6 inches in diameter

1 pea or 1 piece of round corn cereal

When we talk about sizes of heavenly bodies and distances in space, the figures are so enormous that they can be impossible to imagine. In the following activity we have tried to help the children visualize the relative sizes of the nine planets in our solar system.

Before beginning the activity, if you didn't get a chance to read the following book to the children back in February on Copernicus's birthday, now is a great time.

The Magic School Bus Lost in the Solar System by Joanna Cole, Scholastic, 1990.

Another good book on the planets is:

The Picture World of Planets by N. S. Barrett, Franklin Watts, 1990.

1. On a table accessible to all the children, you are going to set up "scale models" of the nine planets. The scale is far from perfect but it is close enough to give the children a good idea of the relative sizes of the nine planets.

2. Explain to the children that the center of our model solar system is empty because even at this tiny scale, we have no ball huge enough to represent our Sun. They will have to imagine an enormous ball, bigger in diameter than the height of a tall basketball player. This enormous ball would be in the center of the table.

   Now add the model planets (each with a name label) one at a time.

3. The closest planet to the Sun is Mercury, which is 3,010 miles (4,850 km) in diameter. In our model Mercury can be represented by a marble (about 1/2 inch in diameter).

4. Second comes Venus and third is Earth. Venus and Earth are almost the same size (Venus—7,520 miles or 12,000 km across, Earth—7,926 miles or 12,756 km in diameter). In our model Venus and Earth can be two golf balls.

5. Mars is quite a bit smaller, 4,220 miles (6,790 km) in diameter. So Mars can be represented by a large "shooter" marble (about 3/4 inch).

6. The next four planets are the big ones. Jupiter is the biggest by far—89,000 miles (143,000 km) in diameter. To represent Jupiter in our model use an inflatable beach ball 15 to 16 inches in diameter. Saturn, next to Jupiter in size (75,000 miles or 120,000 km) can be another beach ball, about 13 inches across. Uranus (32,000 miles, 51,000 km) and Neptune (30,000 miles, 49,000 km) are almost the same size. They can be represented by two cantaloupes or children's rubber balls 5 to 6 inches in diameter.

7. Finally, Pluto is by far the tiniest planet at 1,900 miles or 3,000 km in diameter. It can be represented in our model by a pea or a piece of round corn cereal about 1/4 inch in diameter.

8. When you have put out all your "planets" remind the children that this model does not show the relative distances of the planets from each other. It shows the order of

the planets and their size in comparison with each other.

9. After the children have seen the planets in order, let them move them around. They can rearrange them in order of increasing size and move them to physically compare the relative sizes of different planets. Are they surprised at the vast size difference between the largest and the smallest?

Astronaut Mission Patch

You will need:

Paper

Pencils

Crayons

Plastic lid from margarine or coffee can

Construction paper, any color

Scissors

Markers

Glitter

White craft glue

Safety pin

Masking tape

What would it be like to be an astronaut and go to work in outer space? Here is a book that will give you a good idea of an astronaut's job.

If You Were An Astronaut by Dinah L. Moch, Golden Books, Western, 1985.

Did you know that for every space mission, the astronauts who will be flying the mission design their own official crew patch? For the Apollo XII mission, for example, astronauts Conrad, Gordon, and Bean designed a patch that showed a clipper ship sailing to the moon. (The word "astronaut" is Greek for "sailor to the stars.")

Divide the children into groups of two or three and let each small group design its own patch.

1. Each small group needs some paper, pencils, and crayons. Their first job is to come up with a name for their mission. They can use their school or day care center name or create a name based on their mission goal (e.g., Stargazers, Venus Voyagers). Once the group has agreed upon a name, all the children should draw some very simple designs or pictures to illustrate the mission. (A mission to a planet could be illustrated by a drawing of the planet, another

163

idea could be a few stars, a simple rocket, a moon, etc.) It's important for the children to keep their pictures simple!

2. After they've all done some brainstorming, each group should agree upon one illustration. (This might combine elements of several ideas.) This step may not be easy, but remind the children that astronauts working together do have to cooperate if they want to achieve the mission goals.

3. Now give each child a plastic lid from a margarine tub or coffee can. These will be the backing for their mission patches. Have the children trace around the lids on whatever color construction paper they choose for the background of their patches. Cut out the paper circle, cutting just slightly (about $1/16$ inch) inside the line.

4. Now pass out some markers. Along the top perimeter of the circle, have each child print the mission name in marker. Along the bottom perimeter, all the last names of the "astronauts" in the small group should be printed.

5. Next, within the space left in the middle of the patch, have each child draw and then color in marker the illustration agreed upon by the group. The patches in each group will not be identical because of the individual artists. However, they will all have the same words and hopefully very similar pictures.

6. The colored pictures can be outlined or highlighted with glitter. When they are completed and dry, put a little white craft glue inside the plastic lids and stick the paper circles inside.

7. Attach a safety pin to the back of each lid with a strip of masking tape. Now your "astronauts" can proudly wear their original mission patches.

A Celestial Mobile

You will need:

Wire hangers
Yarn or string
Paper or cardboard
Foil
Newspaper
Masking tape
Markers or paints
Glitter

Let the children create a little bit of the universe to hang in their own rooms with the following activity.

1. Wire hangers are the basic framework for our mobiles. Depending on the age of the children in your group, you can begin with one or more wire hangers for each child. Older children may enjoy taping the top hook of two or three hangers together and then bending the bottom parts of the hangers into a three-dimensional framework.

2. All the children will need yarn or string and materials to create their own heavenly bodies. Here are a few ideas.

   Moons can be full or in any phase down to the narrowest crescent. You can cut out a paper or cardboard moon and paint it (remember our crater paint from the Lunar Art activity) or you can cover the moon with silver foil or glitter. Be creative!

   The Sun and other stars can be created by forming a ball of aluminum foil around the end of a string tied onto the hanger. Or you can form a ball of newspaper and cover it with masking tape, attaching it to the string at the same time. The masking tape can then be painted or colored with markers.

   This same newspaper and masking tape technique can be used for planets. Cardboard rings can be snugly fitted around your newspaper/tape planets too. You can even add spaceships or satellites.

   Attach the heavenly body to a length of string and tie the other end of the string to the wire hanger. You can then slide the string along the hanger to the desired spot.

3. Each child can choose any grouping of heavenly bodies he wants. (Some may just want stars!) Your mobile will be more interesting if you vary both the length of the strings and the sizes of the heavenly bodies. These are also ways to maintain balance in the mobile.

4. The children need a place to hang their mobiles as they work so they can keep them balanced. When they are all completed, display them and see all the different visions of our universe.

165

Amelia Earhart was born on this day in 1897. In 1932 she became the first woman to fly alone across the Atlantic Ocean. Three years later, Earhart soloed across the Pacific from Hawaii to California—again, the first woman to accomplish this feat. In July 1937, Earhart and her navigator set out to attempt the first around-the-world flight by a woman. She never completed this flight—her plane disappeared without a trace. To this day, what really happened on Amelia Earhart's last flight remains a mystery.

Young Amelia Earhart: A Dream to Fly by Susan Alcott, Troll Associates, 1992.

Making Paper Airplanes

Let's remember this brave aviator on her birthday by designing and flying our own paper airplanes.

On the following page, you will find one example of a simple airplane we can make.

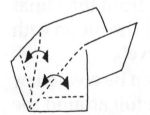 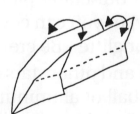 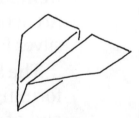

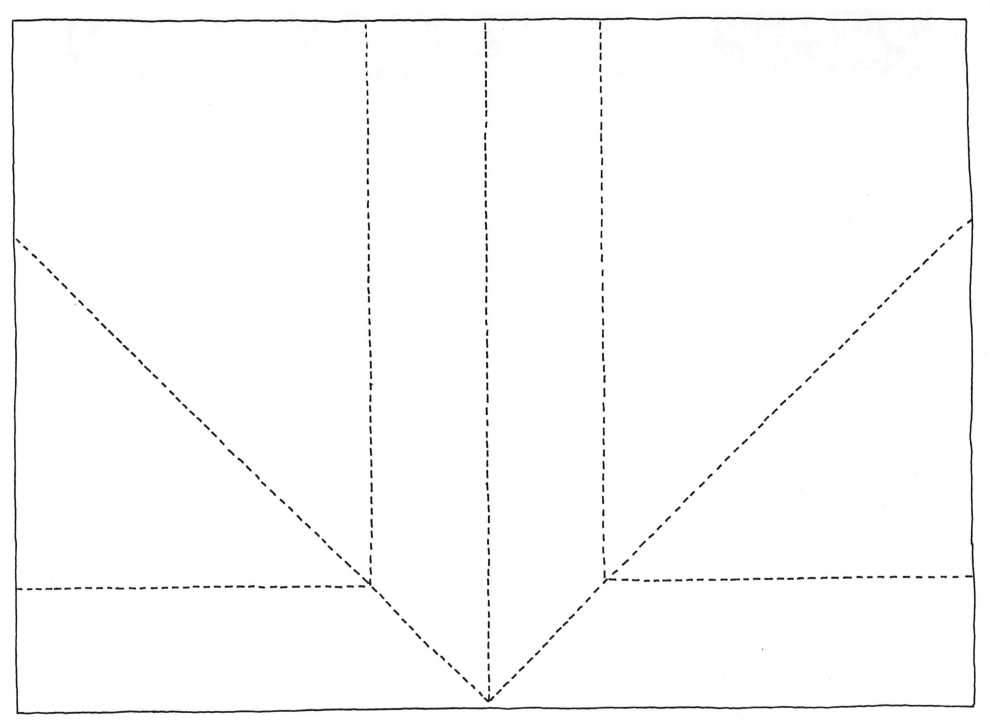

167

JULY IS NATIONAL RECREATION AND PARKS, HOT DOG, BAKED BEAN & ICE-CREAM MONTH

If July brings beautiful summer weather in your neighborhood, you can help the children enjoy it by celebrating all of July's special titles in the next three activities.

Camping Out

You will need:

Tent or large blanket and table

On a beautiful July day, pitch a tent outside. If you have a real tent available by all means use it, but if not, a blanket draped over a picnic table and some benches works just fine.

Let the tent be your home base for the day. Let the children play in it, eat in it, even rest in it on blankets or sleeping bags. Read the children a story in the tent. The following book is perfect for the occasion.

Just Camping Out by Mercer Mayer, Golden Books, Western, 1989.

You may find that even everyday occupations become an adventure for the children when you are out in a tent instead of inside.

A Cookout

In honor of National Hot Dog Month and National Baked Bean Month serve these foods for lunch today. Both can be cooked outside on a grill.

If you are using a charcoal grill allow the fire to burn down to white coals. If you are using a gas grill set it for medium heat. Start with the baked beans.

Baked Beans on the Grill

One 16-ounce can of beans in tomato sauce
1 teaspoon prepared mustard
2 tablespoons brown sugar
Minced onion, if desired

1. In a shallow metal pan mix together the can of beans, mustard, brown sugar, and minced onion.
2. Cover the pan with foil and bake on the grill for about 10 minutes. Then lift one edge of the foil so moisture can escape and bake about 10 more minutes. This recipe serves 5 to 6 children.

Hot Dogs

When your beans have been on for about 10 minutes, let the children cook their hot dogs.

They can put the hot dogs on skewers (or sticks) and carefully hold them over the grill to cook. Have an adult ready to slip the cooked hot dogs into rolls. Then let the children add mustard, ketchup, or relish and some pickles on the side.

Serve lemonade to drink with your hot dogs and beans and for dessert . . .

Homemade Ice Cream

If you have, or can borrow, an ice-cream maker, a hot July day is the perfect time to enjoy some homemade ice cream. It's fun for the children to see how ice cream is made, and most people find the taste of homemade ice cream far surpasses anything we can buy in a store.

Here is a recipe for about 1½ quarts of delicious vanilla ice cream. See your particular ice cream maker for specific directions on how to make it.

Old-Fashioned Vanilla Ice Cream

2 cups (1 pint) heavy cream
2 cups (1 pint) light cream
1 cup sugar
2 teaspoons vanilla extract
⅛ teaspoon salt

Allow about 1 hour for the ice cream to set up. Then serve it and enjoy it, either all by itself or topped with some fresh July fruit!

The beloved children's author, Beatrix Potter, was born in London on July 28, 1866. As an adult, Beatrix wrote a letter to a young friend in which she told and illustrated the story of a naughty bunny. This evolved into her first and most famous book, *The Tale of Peter Rabbit*. This book was followed by many more animal tales, and these same tiny books with beautiful illustrations are charming children today.

"Rabbit" in Sign Language

Cross the hands in front of you with your palms facing your chest. Holding your hands in "U" position (first and second fingers only out straight) curl and uncurl the straight fingers. You are showing the movement of a rabbit's ears.

After the children have mastered the sign, read aloud the following book and let them make the sign whenever you say the word "rabbit."

📖 **The Tale of Peter Rabbit** by Beatrix Potter, Frederick Warne, 1902.

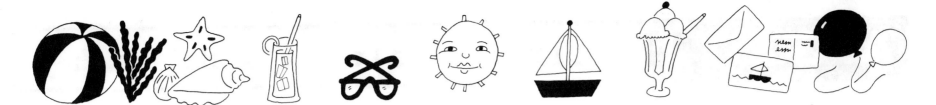

AUGUST

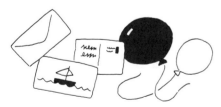
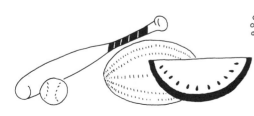

orn in New York City on August 1, 1819, Herman Melville left his home as a young man to be a sailor. His adventurous life included crewing on whaling ships and living on a South Sea jungle island with a tribe of cannibals. He later wrote several novels about his experiences, including his masterpiece, *Moby Dick* or *The White Whale*. A wonderful book all about whales is:

Picture Library: Whales by Norman Barrett, Franklin Watts, 1989.

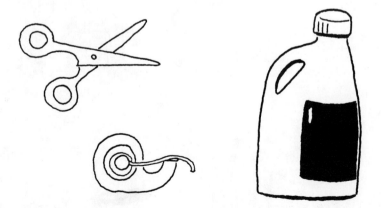

Sailing Ships

You will need:

Plastic laundry detergent bottle
Serrated edge knife
Scissors
3 plastic drinking straws
Clay or Playdoh
Heavy white drawing paper
Hole punch
Tape

The whaling trade of the early nineteenth century was conducted from 100-foot-long, three-masted sailing ships. When a sailor high in the rigging spotted a whale, the actual chase and hunt took place in much smaller boats lowered from the ships.

The following craft can help the children visualize the magnificent sailing ships of the 1800s.

1. Help each child cut a plastic laundry detergent bottle about 4 inches from the bottom. Since the first cut is usually ragged, the child can next trim the bottom piece with scissors until it is $1^1/_2$ to 2 inches on one end, tapering down smoothly to 1 to $1^1/_2$ inches at the other end. This is the hull of the ship; it is higher in front and tapers lower in back.

2. Give each child three drinking straws. These are the three masts. The tallest mast was called the mainmast and was located approximately in the center of the boat. Let each child secure the mainmast in the hull by pressing a small lump of clay or Playdoh in the hull and sticking one end of the straw in it. Then trim $1/_2$ inch off the second straw. This will be the foremast located in front of the mainmast, in the front of the hull. Secure it in clay. Trim 1 inch off the third straw. This is the mizzenmast. Secure it in the back of the hull behind the mainmast.

3. Give each child some heavy white drawing paper. This is the "canvas" for the sails. Whaling ships had square sails instead of triangular ones. This "square rigging" helped keep the tall ship stable in rough seas. Each whaling ship had more than thirty sails. For our models the children can cut six to nine rectangles of varying sizes from the white paper. Holding the long side of each rectangle vertically, use a hole punch to make one hole at the center of the top edge ($1/_2$ inch from the edge) and another hole directly beneath it at the center of the bottom edge.

Thread the sails onto the masts, pushing them down so that they appear to billow in the wind. (If necessary, use a little tape to secure the top sail on each mast.)

Not only do our models serve as reminders of the nineteenth-century whaling days—they actually float!

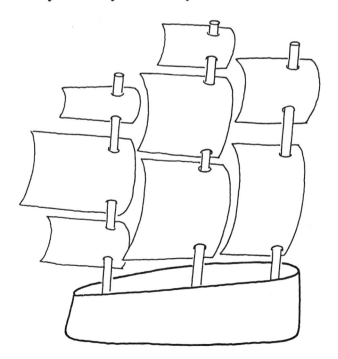

Whale Lovers' Scrimshaw

You will need:

Bar of white soap

Sandpaper or scrub brush

Sharp pencil

Black tempera paint

Paper towel

Nineteenth-century whaling voyages lasted three or four years and longer. In the many weeks between whale sightings, the sailors had long hours without much to do. One of the ways they kept occupied was by carving beautiful objects out of whale's teeth. This delicate art is called scrimshaw.

Today we have become aware that the whaling of the past brought many species of whales to the brink of extinction. Although most countries no longer allow the hunting of whales, we can still appreciate the beauty of the scrimshaw the whalers created.

Show the children some pictures of scrimshaw. For books about scrimshaw, check your local library under "Scrimshaw."

The "scrimshaw" in the following activity is easy to make and friendly to whales!

1. Give each child a bar of white soap. (Ivory soap works well.) Have the children remove the lettering imprinted on the soap either by lightly sanding it or by scrubbing it with a scrub brush. Then have them run it through their hands under water to smooth out the surface.

2. If you carve in the soap while it is still damp, press very lightly. Using a sharp pencil, draw a simple picture on the bar of soap. As you draw the pencil point is engraving the soap.

3. When you are finished drawing, brush black tempera paint across the entire surface on which you drew. Then with a damp paper towel gently wipe off the paint on the uncut surface. Keep wiping until the uncut surface is pure white again. The lines you engraved with the pencil should stay black. Nineteenth-century whalers often darkened the lines they engraved with tobacco juice!

4. You can repeat steps 2 and 3 until you are satisfied with your "scrimshaw." Then let it dry.

Sailor's Knots

You will need:

4- to 6-foot lengths of twine

Stick or dowel rod at least 6 inches long

Tape

Beads (optional)

Another way the sailors passed their spare time on long whaling voyages was in working fancy knots in lengths of rope or cord. Certainly knotting skill was needed in securing the rigging. However, the sailors also produced decorative pieces of knotting, which were known as "McNamara's Lace." Today we call this kind of knotting macrame (pronounced mac´rah may). For an introduction to this craft, check your local library under "Macrame."

A macrame wall hanging is a simple way to learn and practice this decorative knotting technique.

You will need a stick or dowel rod for each child (at least 6 inches long) and some cord. Mason's twine, available at hardware stores, works well.

1. For each child, cut four 6-foot lengths of twine. These will be folded in half producing eight 3-foot cords to knot.

2. The first step the children need to do is to mount their twine on the sticks. Have them fold each piece of twine in half. Bring the loop of the fold-point over the top of the stick. Then pull the two cut ends of the twine through the loop until the twine is snugly knotted to the stick. Do this to each piece of twine.

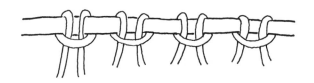

3. Any macrame book can show you how to tie and combine many different knots. For simplicity's sake we are offering instructions on two basic kinds: the double half-hitch and the square knot. By combining these two knots in different ways, the children can make attractive wall hangings with minimal skill. Of course, interested children should be directed to reference books for additional instruction.

The Double Half-Hitch

1. For this knot you need a "holding cord"; i.e., a cord that you will knot the other cords onto. Take your first cord on the left and hold it to the right, across and on top of the other seven cords and parallel to the stick. To secure the holding cord, tape both the left and right sides of the cord to the table even with the two ends of the stick and about 2 inches down from the stick. Keep the holding cord taut.

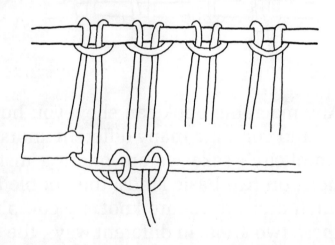

2. Take the next cord and bring it over the holding cord and then behind the holding cord and out through the loop that is formed.

Pull the "knot" tight, then bring the end of the same cord back up over the holding cord and behind again, to the left of the knot you just made, and pull it out through the loop. Pull tight.

3. If you continue the instructions in step 2 for all the cords you will have a double half-hitch row. These rows can also be formed at an angle by keeping the holding cord at an angle.

The Square Knot

1. The square knot uses four cords. You work the first and fourth cords over two stationary middle cords. While you are learning, tuck the last four cords on the stick out of the way, to avoid confusion.

2. From left to right, let's call the four cords A, B, C, and D. Take cord A, and pull it over cords B and C and under cord D.

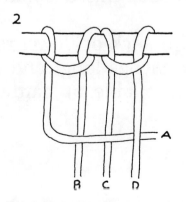

3. Then take cord D and pull it under cords C and B and over cord A (through the loop between B and A).

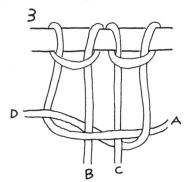

4. Next take cord A (now at the far right) and bring it over cords C and B and under cord D.

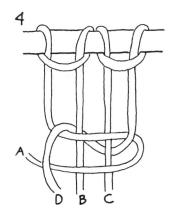

5. Finally, take cord D (now at the far left) under B and C and over A (through the loop again). Pull tight and you have a square knot.

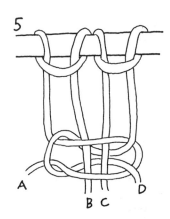

6. Many different patterns can be formed using the square knot. After making a few on the left and then the right, you can leave the first two and last two cords on the stick unknotted and just work the center four.

Remember to encourage the children to be creative mixing the knots. They can get plenty of ideas from books on macrame. The children should feel free to add beads, additional sticks, anything they can think of to make their wall hangings special and unique.

When you look at all the different macrame designs you have created, remember the whalers who passed this art on to us.

Undersea Art

You will need:

Reference books with pictures of undersea life
1 piece of light blue posterboard
1 piece of construction paper (same size as posterboard, contrasting color)
Ruler
Pencil
Crayons or markers
Scraps of construction paper
Colored paper
Scraps of colored tissue
Scissors
Glue
Sand, small shells
Green plastic wrap
Masking tape

Melville and the whalers sailed over the ocean's surface but deep beneath that surface is an entirely different world. The plant and animal life of that undersea world is often like nothing on earth!

Share some pictures of undersea life with the children. There are some beautiful ones in the following book.

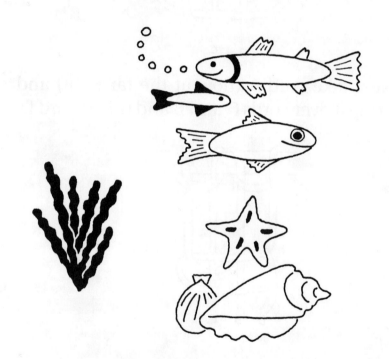

The Sea (The World Around Us series) by Brian Williams, Warwick Press, 1991.

Now let the children have some fun creating their own interpretations of the undersea world!

1. Give each child a piece of light blue poster-board and a piece of construction paper of equal size (in a contrasting color). Have the children use a ruler to draw a 1½-inch margin all around the posterboard. Remind them to leave this margin blank.

2. Bring out the pencils, crayons, markers, scraps of construction paper and colored tissue, scissors, and glue. Let the children draw sea creatures and plants on colored paper and cut them out. It may be helpful to have a few picture reference books handy for the children to look at. Here are some suggestions of sea life you may want to include: fish, eels, shellfish, sea stars, jelly-fish, coral, seaweed, squid, and octopus. And don't forget marine mammals—whales, dolphins, and porpoises.

3. On the posterboard have the children draw a wave line to indicate the top of the ocean just a little below the top margin. Then let them arrange all their sea life and glue it on. (Marine mammals come out of the ocean to breathe. One of them could be half in and half out of the water.)

4. On the floor of the ocean the children can glue sand and some small shells. Let all the glue dry completely.

5. To add a watery texture to the pictures, give each child some green plastic wrap (available in food stores). Scrunch up the plastic wrap a little so that it looks like rippling water. Cover the underwater part of the pictures with the plastic wrap, attaching it with masking tape in the margins.

6. The construction paper is for a frame. Have the children fold it in half and cut out a 2-inch wide square "U" shape (the top of the "U" is on the fold of the paper). Open up the paper and glue it over the margin, framing your undersea artwork.

Peace Day, every August 6, helps us to remember a tragic day in our history. On August 6, 1945, the first atomic bomb was dropped on the city of Hiroshima, Japan. We commemorate this anniversary not just to remember the past, but to commit ourselves to a peaceful future for our world.

The following book talks about Peace Day in Japan. It is a sad story but a true one and may help older children understand what Peace Day is all about.

Sadako and the Thousand Paper Cranes by Eleanor Coerr, Dell, 1977.

In Japan, folded paper cranes have become a symbol of peace. The following two activities show you how to make two other peace symbols.

Doves for Peace

You will need:

- Pencil
- Cardboard
- Glue
- White felt
- Scissors
- Fiberfill
- Straight pins
- Colored embroidery thread
- Needle

Because of its gentle nature, the dove has long been a symbol of peace. With white felt, embroidery thread, and fiberfill, the children can make beautiful doves.

1. For your dove you can use the flying bird pattern used in the Making Flying Birds activity or draw your own simple silhouette of a dove. Mount it on cardboard and let the children trace it onto two pieces of white felt.

Since the white felt is easily soiled, make sure the children have clean hands and a clean work area. Have them cut out their two doves.

2. Give each child a little fiberfill (available in any craft store) and some straight pins. Let them pin their two doves together, adding just a little fiberfill in between to make the dove three dimensional.

3. Now let the children select a color of embroidery thread. They will use it to stitch their doves together and to sew on an eye.

4. To sew the doves together, show the children how to do an overcast stitch. Have them take stitches over the edge of the felt. By holding their needle at a slant, the stitches will appear on an angle. Older children can try to keep the stitches at an equal depth and evenly spaced.

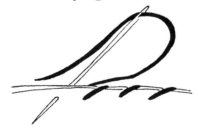

5. When the doves are sewn together, add their eyes with French knots. First have the children knot the ends of the thread on their needles and bring the thread through the felt where they want the eyes to be. (This knot becomes one eye.) Then have them hold the thread a few inches from the felt with the left hand and wind the thread twice around the needle. Still holding the thread taut, twist the needle back to the starting point and insert it close to the point from which it came out before. Pull all the thread through and secure in the back. (This becomes the other eye.)

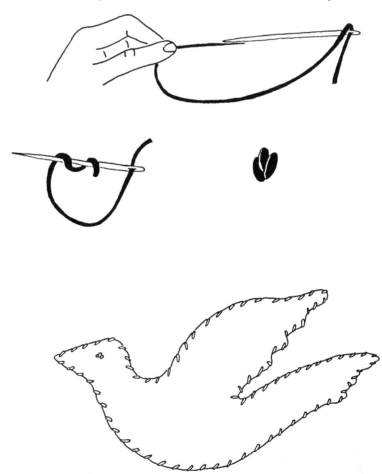

A Modern Peace Symbol

You will need:

Plastic lid from a 1-pound coffee can
Marker
Scissors
Yarn

There is another peace symbol, which many of the children may recognize. They can make one with a plastic lid and some yarn.

1. Give each child a plastic lid from a one-pound coffee can. With a wide tip marker, draw a circle around the perimeter of the lid and then draw a "Y" that touches the circle at its three outer points. Continue the bottom stem of the "Y" until it touches the edge of the circle.

2. Have the children carefully cut out the negative space between the lines they drew. Turn the lid around so that the "Y" is upside down. Do they recognize it?

3. Now let each child choose some yarn in one or more colors. Have them wind the yarn around the circle and the "Y," completely covering the plastic. Tie off the yarn and tuck in the ends.

Another piece of yarn can be tied on as a hanger.

4. Display your peace symbol if you want to express the hope that is engraved on the statue of Sadako in Hiroshima Peace Park.

This is our cry,
this is our prayer;
peace in the world.

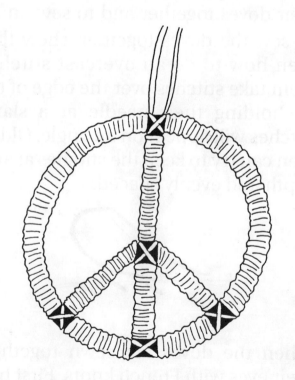

AUGUST 11 | Alex Haley's Birthday

Alex Palmer Haley was born in Ithaca, New York, August 11, 1921. Although Haley's first book, *The Autobiography of Malcolm X*, was a bestseller, he is most famous for his Pulitzer Prize—winning novel, *Roots*. Haley was raised by his grandmother in Tennessee, and *Roots* was based upon his own family history as related by his grandmother and great aunts and researched by the author.

Explore Your Roots

You will need:

Copy of the following illustration

When *Roots* was published in 1976, it inspired many people to investigate their ancestry. In honor of Alex Haley's birthday, help the children complete their own family trees.

1. Make a copy of the tree on the following page for each child.

2. Have each child fill in the names of his or her mother (maiden name), maternal grandparents, and maternal great-grandparents on one side of the tree. The father's name, paternal grandparents' and great-grandparents' names can be written on the other side. (Do the children know what "maternal" and "paternal" mean?) This step may well involve some parental input and can often generate some interesting family discussions.

183

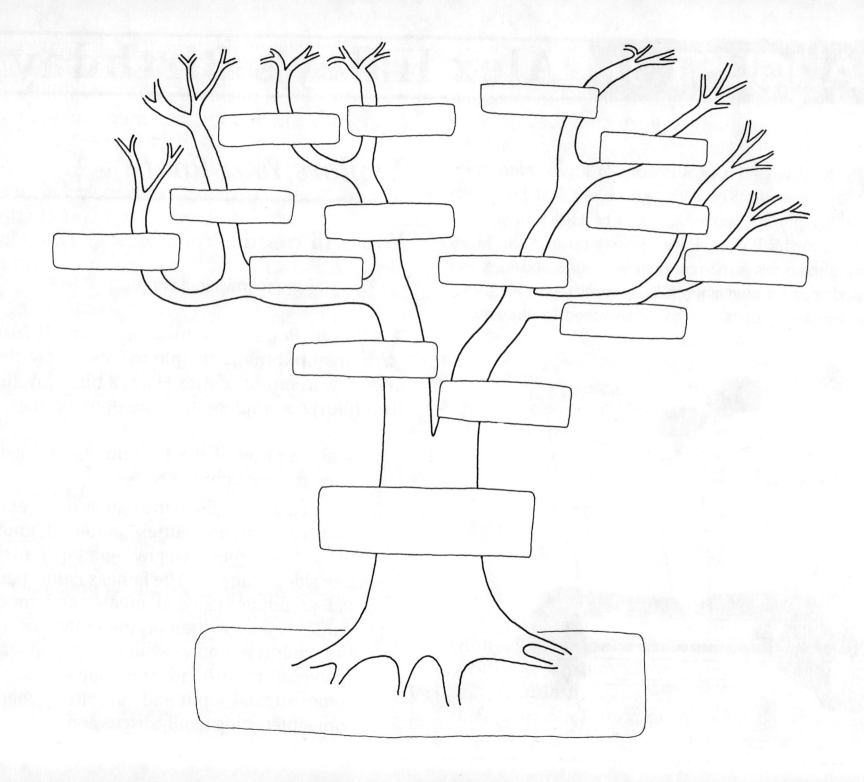

3. Children who were adopted can use the tree for the information on their adoptive family. In the space at the roots of the tree, they can write in any information they have on their biological family, i.e., names and/or country of origin for children adopted from another country.

4. When the family trees are all filled in, the children can color them. They should be encouraged to keep them and perhaps to try to learn a little bit about the people on their trees.

A Family Portrait

You will need:

1 sheet of drawing paper

Pencil

Crayons or markers

Generally, when we say the word "family," children think first about the family they live with. Today, more than ever, these families come in a variety of configurations. A cartoon family portrait is fun for children to make and becomes a good starting point for a discussion of what makes a family.

1. Give each child a sheet of drawing paper and a pencil and have them draw a cartoon portrait of the family with whom they live. They should include themselves in the portrait. After it is drawn, the portrait can be colored.

2. If a child's parents live apart and he or she lives with both families some of the time, encourage the child to draw two family portraits.

3. When the drawings are finished, have the children title their portraits by their family names, e.g., "The Smith Family." Then display all the portraits around the room.

4. Talk about all the different kinds of families portrayed.

   What, if anything, do all these families have in common?

   After your discussion, here is a book you may enjoy.

Families Are Different by Nina Pellegrini, Holiday House, 1991.

Many communities hold baby parades, but every year on the second Thursday in August America's oldest baby parade is held in Ocean City, New Jersey. Every year since the turn of the century, Ocean City's babies have been strolled down the boardwalk in carriages, wagons, and floats.

On the anniversary of this annual event, have some fun with your "babies" with the following activity.

A Baby Picture Parade

You will need:

Baby picture of the child
1 sheet of construction paper
2 pieces of wagon wheel macaroni
Plastic coffee can lid
Pencil
Scissors
Glue
Tape

1. Have the children bring in baby pictures of themselves, each in an envelope. They should not show anyone in the group their pictures.

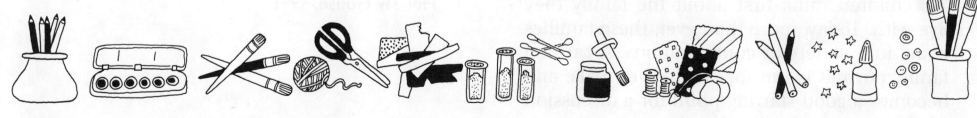

2. Give every child a sheet of construction paper and two pieces of wagon wheel macaroni. The first job is to make baby carriages.

3. Have the children trace a circle around a plastic coffee can lid on the construction paper. Then have them cut the circle out, fold it in half, open it, and cut on the fold line.

4. Have the children lay the two half circles down, fitting the two halves back into a circle shape with the cut horizontal. Let them turn the top half to the left until the straight edge is vertical. This is the back of the baby carriage. Glue the two halves together at the lower left where they overlap. Then glue the two "wheels" to the bottom of the carriage.

5. Now the children are on the honor system not to peek at anyone else's work. The children should tuck their baby pictures behind the carriages so that the baby shows. Have them attach the picture with some tape on the back, then turn the carriage over so no one can see the picture.

6. Come around with a bag or box to collect the baby carriages. Mix them up and then hang them up in a long, single file parade. Let everyone have some fun guessing which baby is who!

The decade of the sixties certainly had a style all its own, and what better time to celebrate that style than on the anniversary of the Woodstock Music and Art Fair.

On August 14–16, 1969, on a farm near Woodstock, New York, over half a million people gathered to listen to music. Forever after, the Woodstock Festival has remained a symbol of the rock-and-roll generation of the sixties.

The following pictorial book gives a great look at what life in the sixties was like.

Life: The 60's edited by Doris C. O'Neil, A Bulfinch Press Book, Little, Brown, 1989.

Tie-Dyeing

You will need:

Clean white or light-colored T-shirt
A lot of rubber bands or twine
Rubber gloves
Several pots or buckets (2-gallon size),
   1 for each color dye you are using
Fabric dye in several colors
Mild detergent
Water
Smock to protect clothes

Help the children make a fashion statement, sixties style, by creating their own tie-dyed T-shirts.

Every child needs a clean white or light-colored T-shirt, a lot of rubber bands or twine, and a pair of rubber gloves (disposable surgical gloves are fine).

The group needs several large (at least 2-gallon) pots or buckets. You will need one bucket for each color of dye you are using, plus two additional buckets. (Be aware that plastic buckets will probably be stained by the dye.)

The group also needs fabric dye in several colors. If you use liquid dye instead of powdered, you can dilute it in hot tap water rather than boiling water. This may be a safer choice for working with children.

1. Prepare the dye. Dilute it in hot water at double the recommended strength on the package directions. (For example, our dye package recommended 1/2 cup dye to 3 gallons hot water, so we used 1/2 cup dye to 1 1/2 gallons water.) This will give you vivid colors and fast results.

   When preparing and using the dye be careful not to splash it. It will stain. Use smocks and rubber gloves and protect the work area.

   When the dye is prepared, fill an empty bucket with warm water and a little mild detergent. Fill another bucket with plain cool water.

2. Prepare the shirts. All the shirts should be wet before they are dyed, so have the children soak them in plain water and wring them out. Then start tying.

You will be bunching fabric together and securing it tightly with twine or rubber bands. If you tie it tightly enough, the places it is tied will not absorb any dye. According to how you bundle the fabric, you can make different patterns.

For a sunburst effect, pinch a piece of fabric and pull up. Tie off the fabric you pulled up in one or more places. If you are trying a design of several colors, start with the palest color of dye and progress to the darkest last.

You can twist a section of fabric and secure the twists with twine or rubber bands.

You can achieve a marbleized effect by bunching up the fabric in a ball and crisscrossing the bundle with twine or rubber bands.

When you've tied in your designs, you are ready to dye.

3. Using rubber gloves to protect your hands, dip the part of the shirt you are dyeing in the desired color. Leave it in the dye bath for 10 to 15 minutes. If you are making a multicolored design, when the time is up, squeeze out the fabric and dip it into the next color for another 10 to 15 minutes.

4. When you are finished dyeing and before you untie, immerse your fabric in the bucket of warm soapy water. Then rinse well in cool, clear water. Continue rinsing until the water runs clear.
5. Finally, remove the ties and take a look at the far-out designs you created. Your T-shirts can be dried on a clothesline or in a dryer.

Love Beads

You will need:

24- to 36-inch piece of yarn
Uncooked macaroni (any shape you can thread)
Food coloring
Rubbing alcohol
Paper towels

Love beads were worn by people of both sexes in the sixties.

1. First the children need to dye their macaroni "beads." For each color desired, put about 1 cup of rubbing alcohol in a shallow container. Add a few drops food coloring and mix. Then drop in the macaroni and leave it until it is the shade you want. Dry macaroni on paper towels. Remember, some macaroni can be left its natural color.
2. Next, have them thread their "beads" on the yarn in any pattern (or no pattern) they want. If they tie a knot around the first piece of macaroni they thread, at one end of the string, it may make the rest of the job easier.
3. When the children are finished, help them tie their necklaces closed. Wearing their tie-dyed T-shirts and love beads, they'll be dressed perfectly for the next two activities.

A Sixties Snack

The granola bars we eat today got their start in a favorite food of the sixties—granola. Here's a recipe for some groovy granola that's actually nutritious as well as delicious.

1/2 cup honey
8 cups rolled oats
2 cups toasted wheat germ
1/2 cup chopped peanuts
1/2 cup sunflower seeds
2 cups raisins
1 envelope (to make 1 quart) nonfat dry milk

1. Heat the honey at low heat until it is very liquid. Mix with rolled oats, stirring until oats are completely coated with honey.
2. Spread honey-coated oats in shallow cookie trays and toast in the oven at 300°F. Stir every 5 to 10 minutes. Bake until golden brown. Remove from oven and let cool.
3. In a large bowl, mix toasted oats with remaining ingredients. Stir until all ingredients are thoroughly blended.
4. Enjoy with milk or plain.

A Sign of the Sixties

Here is a sixties song from "Woodstock" by Joni Mitchell.

By the time we got to Woodstock
We were half a million strong.
Everywhere was a song and a celebration.
And I dreamed I saw the bombers
Riding shotgun in the skies
turning into butterflies
above our nation.

Certainly the "establishment" rejected by the youth of the sixties included the military establishment. The "ban the bomb" generation had their own special "sign language," the peace sign.

With your palms facing away from you, hold up your index and middle fingers, forming a "V." Your thumb is curled around the fourth and fifth fingers.

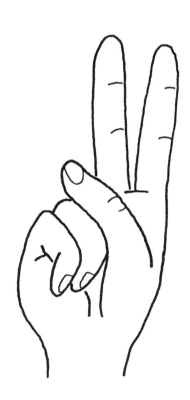

Your history books may have told you that the transcontinental railroad was completed at the town of Promontory Point, Utah. However, true railroad buffs know that the eastward and westward tracks actually met more than a year later outside the town of Comanche, Colorado (now called Strasburg) on August 15, 1870. Every August, Strasburg proudly remembers this historic anniversary, and the next two activities can get the children in the spirit of the occasion.

Trains: The History of Railroads by David Jefferis, Franklin Watts, 1991.

Playing Train

You will need:

A few chairs

Counter or desk

Index cards cut in half

Hats

Hole punch

Sound effects (maracas, shakers, etc.)

Play money or chips

This is great fun for young children.

1. Make a long line of chairs, a few more chairs than you have children. This is your train.
2. You will need a ticket agent to sell the tickets, a conductor to punch the tickets, and an engineer to drive the train. The rest of the children are passengers. Every trip, the roles can be changed.

3. You need a few simple props. The ticket agent needs a place to sell tickets, i.e., a counter, desk, etc., and some tickets (index cards cut in half work fine).

   The conductor and the engineer both need hats; use any cap but let the children make a paper insignia patch that they can staple or tape to the front of the hat.

   The conductor needs a paper punch and the engineer is in charge of sound effects, so if you have any shakers or maracas, give them to the engineer.

   The passengers need some play money or chips to buy their tickets.

4. To begin play the passengers should line up to buy their tickets. Let them think of destinations for their trips so they know what tickets they want. Do they know what "one-way" and "round-trip" mean?

5. After they purchase tickets, the passengers can choose their seats. (The front seat is reserved for the engineer.) The conductor calls, "All aboard!"

6. You know the train is on its way when the engineer "blows the whistle." The engineer also makes the train "chug-chug" along the tracks. As you travel, the conductor comes along and punches everyone's ticket.

To pass the time on your journey, you may even want to sing "I've Been Working on the Railroad."

7. When you arrive, the engineer stops the train, and the passengers depart. Exchange your props and you're on your way again.

Cooperative Train Craft

You will need:

1 long piece of computer paper
Crayons or markers
Construction paper
Scissors
Cotton
Glue
Wagon wheel macaroni
"Freight"
–pictures from old magazines
–gravel, sand, beans
–pretzel sticks, candies
–pennies, buttons, etc.

Now that you have all ridden a passenger train, work together to build a freight train.

1. Lay a long piece of computer paper on the floor. Make it long enough for all the children to work on it comfortably. Along the bottom of the paper draw a railroad track with a black crayon or marker.

2. You can make a simple engine to pull the train. Cut out a construction paper rectangle about 5 by 2 inches. Next cut out two right triangles with 1½-inch sides at the right angle. Add one triangle to the bottom front of the "engine." This is your "cow catcher." (Do the children know what this was used for?) Add the other triangle with the point overlapping the top edge of the engine. This is the smokestack. You can even add cotton smoke puffing out.

3. Now let every child choose a piece of construction paper and cut out a rectangle about 5 by 2 inches. Let the children each glue two wagon wheel macaroni on the rectangle as wheels. Then let them glue the cars onto the railroad track.

4. Here are a few suggestions for loading the freight train. Choose the one you think will work best for the children.

   • You can glue real objects on top of the cars. You might use gravel, buttons, pennies, cotton balls, beans, candies, tiny pretzel sticks, etc. It's fun to work with real "freight."

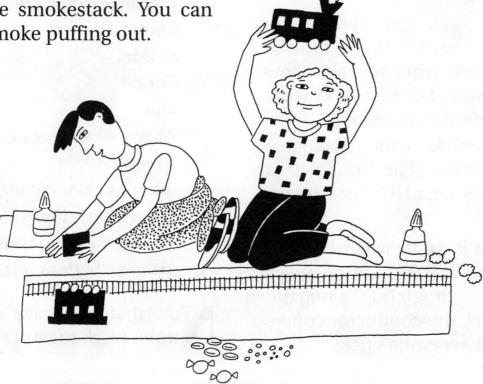

- The children can look through magazines and cut out pictures of objects in one category to glue in their cars. For example, they could choose pictures of animals, food, toys, furniture, etc. This helps a child categorize and also understand that trains transport all kinds of things.

- Young children might want to cut out pictures that match the colors of their train cars so that you end up with a color train in which the red car carries red objects, the green car carries only green things, etc.

5. When all the cars are on the track and loaded, use your crayon or marker to draw lines hooking the cars together.

6. Finally, make a red caboose to complete the train. Out of red construction paper cut three rectangles, one 5 by 2 inches, one 1/2 by 6 inches, and one 1 by 2 inches. The 5-by-2-inch rectangle is the body of your caboose. Glue the 1/2-by-6-inch rectangle on top as a roof. The 1-by-2-inch rectangle goes on top of the middle of the roof as a cupola. You can draw windows on the caboose since this is the car in which the train crew rest and eat.

While you are waiting for the glue to dry, here's a classic train story to enjoy with the children.

The Little Engine That Could by Watty Piper, Platt, 1961.

When it's time to hang up your train, let everyone help! Display it proudly in honor of the real completion of the U.S. Transcontinental Railroad!

AUGUST 27 — Mother Teresa's Birthday

Agnes Gonxha Bojaxhiu was born on August 27, 1910 in Skopie, Yugoslavia.

As a young woman, Agnes became a nun, taking the name Teresa, and went to work as a missionary in India. There, Sister Teresa left her teaching job to work with the poor and homeless. She and the nuns who work with her live as simply as the people they serve. In 1979 Mother Teresa received a great honor—the Nobel Peace Prize for her loving work with the poor. Today the work of Mother Teresa's Missionaries of Charity is going on all over the world.

An inspiring account of Mother Teresa's life to read to the children is:

📖 ***Mother Teresa, Friend of the Friendless*** by Carol Greene, Childrens Press, 1983.

Friends in Need

Mother Teresa has been called "the friend of the friendless." Why not honor the birthday of this great woman by taking the time to be a friend to the friendless in your neighborhood.

Here are a few friendly suggestions:

1. Collect canned food and/or good used clothing. Bring it to a local shelter, church, or charitable agency for distribution to those who need it.
2. Visit a local nursing home (see Fourth Sunday in September—Good Neighbor Day).
3. Send a card, note, or picture to someone who is ill, shut in, or just lonely. Knowing he or she is remembered can really brighten a person's day.

We don't have to go to India to be a friend to others. We can start right where we are.

Have you or anyone you know attended a Montessori school? These schools were named for the Italian educator, Maria Montessori born on this day in 1870. Maria Montessori believed that children learn best when they make use of real learning experiences in their everyday world. Her method of teaching has influenced education everywhere.

Celebrate the birthday of this famous educator by enjoying the following activity.

Fraction Fun

Let the children enjoy a hands-on "math lesson" with the following activity.

You will need:

Playdoh or clay

Rolling pin

Pizza cutters

Round cookie cutter or cup

Sandwich fixings

Apples

1. Let the children roll out dough and cut into circles.
2. Let them use the pizza cutters to cut their circles into halves, quarters, eighths, etc. (To make thirds, sixths, etc., let them cut a wide "Y" shape in their circles.)
3. Let the children cut some sandwiches into fractions and share them with a friend. Share apple halves or quarters, too! Can they see how we use fractions every day? **197**

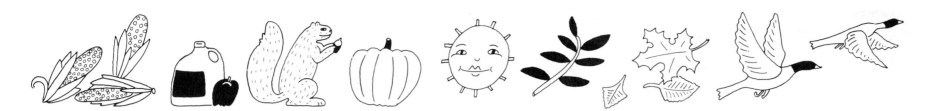

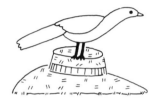

SEPTEMBER

Labor Day

If you work and live in the United States, Canada, or Puerto Rico, the first Monday every September is your holiday! Since 1884, Labor Day has been a U.S. national holiday, set aside to honor all working people.

To commemorate Labor Day, talk with the children about work and jobs and how everyone has a job. What about the children—do they have a job? If a mother stays home, does she have a job? Here are two books for young children to help stimulate this discussion.

He Bear, She Bear by Stan and Jan Berenstain, Random House, 1974.

Maybe You Should Fly a Jet! Maybe You Should Be a Vet! by Theodore LeSieg, Random House, 1980.

Job Charades

You will need:

Any prop that can represent a job

Children of any age can enjoy this activity. One child stands in front of the group and acts out a job using no words. The other children have to guess the job. Everyone gets a turn performing a charade.

Younger children may use a prop (a pencil for a writer, a wrench for a plumber). Some children may want to act out a parent's job or the job they want to do when they grow up.

Hopefully, by the end of this activity, the children will have a better idea of the enormous variety of jobs that people do.

 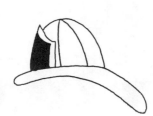     

SEPTEMBER 7 | Grandma Moses's Birthday

If you ever thought you were too old to try something new, think of Grandma Moses. Born September 7, 1860, Anna Mary Robertson grew up to be a hard working farmer's wife who did not begin painting until she was in her late seventies. Before she died, at over a hundred years of age, Grandma Moses's simple "primitive" country scenes had been exhibited throughout the world.

Paint a "Primitive" Scene

You will need:

Art paper
Pencils
Paints

Show the children prints of some of Grandma Moses's paintings. Then pass out some art paper, pencils, and paints. Instruct the children to draw and then paint their own pictures. To help them paint in Grandma Moses's style, have them keep the following points in mind as they work.

1. Keep the work very basic. Young children will do this naturally. Remind older ones that in primitive painting a flat, decorative quality is desired. Don't worry about shading and three-dimensionality.

2. Keep your colors bright and cheerful. Tempera or poster paints would be a good choice. Grandma Moses painted in oils.

3. For the subject matter think of your neighborhood. All Grandma Moses's paintings give a sense of her community, rural upstate New York. Let your paintings give their viewers a sense of your community (e.g., your neighborhood, school, playground, park, etc.)

4. When the paintings are dry, hang them for your own art exhibit. If you are this good now, just think what gifted artists you will be with another seventy years' practice!

The United Nations has declared September 8 to be International Literacy Day. Do the children know what "literacy" means? Do they understand why it is so important? Imagine together a grown-up's day and all the many times reading is required. Think of street signs, newspapers, mail, medicine bottles, instructions and recipes, helping children with homework, reading stories to children.

If the children think that here in the United States illiteracy is not a problem, they need to think again. According to the Literacy Volunteers of America, one out of five adults in the United States is functionally illiterate.

"Read" Around the World

In the spirit of international literacy, help the children learn to say "read" in seven languages (French, Spanish, Russian, German, Japanese, Korean, and Swahili).

French	LIRE (leer)
Spanish	LEER (lay-air)
Russian	(chee-tot´)
German	LESSEN (lay-zen)
Japanese	(yoh-moo)
Korean	(ilk-da)
Swahili	(so-mah)

After learning how to say "read" as they do in different countries, why not read some folktales or fairy tales from around the world. Just look on the library shelves under J398.2. Stories from other lands can offer children insights into different cultures and may open some interesting discussions too.

Library Cards

What better way to spend International Literacy Day than by reading? And what better place to find something good to read than at the local library—so stop in with the children.

The American Library Association has declared September to be "Library Card Sign-Up Month." If the children have library cards, they should bring them and use them. If they do not have library cards and they are eligible for them, this is the perfect time to sign up.

For those who need help finding a book that interests them, refer to the You Can Learn Anything at Your Library activity.

For many children in the United States, Labor Day signals the end of summer vacation and a return to school. Since a lot of these children will be walking to school or to their bus stops, this is a great time to talk about school bus and traffic safety, especially with young children. The next four activities can help you instill these principles and have some fun at the same time.

School Bus Safety

Do any of the children in your group ride school buses? If so, take some time to talk about school bus safety.

The following very simple book is a good place to start. Use the pictures to help illustrate the safety tips below.

School Bus by Donald Crews, Scholastic, 1984.

1. Bus Stop Behavior
   –Be there on time.
   –Stay out of the street while waiting.
2. Getting on and off the Bus
   –If you have to cross the street, always cross in front of the bus.
   –Be sure you are far enough in front of the bus for the driver to see you.
   –Wait until the bus is completely stopped before approaching it or getting out of your seat.

–Use the handrail when getting on or off the bus.

3. On the Bus
   –Stay seated whenever the bus is moving.
   –Talk quietly. If it is too noisy, the driver cannot concentrate.
   –Keep the aisles clear.
   –Keep head, arms, etc., inside the bus and not hanging out the windows.
   –ALWAYS obey the bus driver. The driver's rules are for your safety.

Traffic Light Craft

You will need:

Egg carton
Pencil
Yarn (about 18 inches long)
Small scraps of red, yellow, and green
    construction paper
Scissors
Glue

Help the children make their own traffic lights, which they can use again in the following activities.

1. For each child, cut a piece of an egg carton that has three egg cups in a vertical row. With a sharp pencil, let them poke two holes side by side in the top egg cup. (When the traffic lights are finished, the children can thread yarn through the holes and wear the traffic lights around their necks.)

2. Give the children small scraps of red, yellow, and green construction paper. Let them trace circles about the size of a quarter in each color and cut them out.

3. Let the children put a drop of glue on the bottom of each egg cup and then glue on their traffic lights. The red light goes on top (on the egg cup with the holes), the yellow in the middle, green on the bottom.

4. When the glue is dry, help each child thread a piece of yarn (about 18 inches long) through the holes in the egg cup. Hang the traffic light in the center of the yarn and tie the ends together. The traffic light can be worn for the next two activities.

Traffic Light Song

A wonderful kindergarten teacher we know teaches this song to her students every year. If it's new to you, we think you'll find it an enjoyable way for the children to learn traffic safety. Music notations are indicated above the words.

Ⓖ Ⓔ Ⓔ Ⓖ Ⓖ   Ⓒ
I SAW A BIG RED LIGHT!

Ⓕ Ⓓ Ⓕ Ⓕ   Ⓑ
I SAW A BIG RED LIGHT!

Ⓖ Ⓔ Ⓔ Ⓖ Ⓖ   Ⓒ
I SAW A BIG RED LIGHT

Ⓓ Ⓕ Ⓔ Ⓓ   Ⓒ
ON MY WAY TO SCHOOL.

Ⓖ Ⓖ Ⓖ   Ⓔ   Ⓔ   Ⓖ   Ⓖ   Ⓒ
THE BIG RED LIGHT MEANS STOP! STOP! STOP!

Ⓕ Ⓕ Ⓕ   Ⓓ   Ⓓ   Ⓕ   Ⓕ   Ⓑ
THE BIG RED LIGHT MEANS STOP! STOP! STOP!

Ⓖ Ⓖ Ⓖ   Ⓔ   Ⓔ   Ⓖ   Ⓖ   Ⓒ
THE BIG RED LIGHT MEANS STOP! STOP! STOP!

Ⓓ Ⓕ Ⓔ Ⓓ Ⓒ
ON MY WAY TO SCHOOL.
(repeat)

I SAW A YELLOW LIGHT
I SAW A YELLOW LIGHT
I SAW A YELLOW LIGHT
ON MY WAY TO SCHOOL.

THE YELLOW LIGHT MEANS SLOW DOWN
THE YELLOW LIGHT MEANS SLOW DOWN
THE YELLOW LIGHT MEANS SLOW DOWN
ON MY WAY TO SCHOOL.

I SAW A BIG GREEN LIGHT
I SAW A BIG GREEN LIGHT
I SAW A BIG GREEN LIGHT
ON MY WAY TO SCHOOL.

THE BIG GREEN LIGHT MEANS GO! GO! GO!
THE BIG GREEN LIGHT MEANS GO! GO! GO!
THE BIG GREEN LIGHT MEANS GO! GO! GO!
ON MY WAY TO SCHOOL.

If the children are wearing their traffic lights, let them point to the appropriate one as they sing.

Traffic Light Game

This game is a fun combination of "Red Light, Green Light" and "Mother May I."

1. Have the children wear the traffic lights they made in the Traffic Light Craft activity.

2. Each child gets a turn to be the traffic light. That child stands on one side of the room or yard. All the other children stand side by side in a line on the other side of the room or yard and facing the "traffic light."

3. The children in the line will move toward the "traffic light." Whoever gets there first tags the "light" and then gets a turn to be "traffic light." How the children move is dictated by the "traffic light." He or she can tell them to hop on one foot, jog, skip, walk, etc. The "traffic light" also controls when the children stop and go. If he or she calls out "red light," the children must stop. "Green light" lets the children go again. If the "traffic light" is wearing a traffic light necklace, he or she can cover the other two lights with a hand so that only the appropriate light is showing.

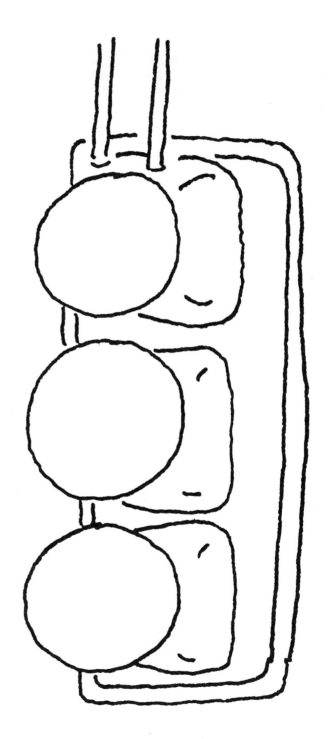

Every year, during the second week of September, the largest Native American fair, the Navajo Nation Fair, is held in Window Rock, Arizona. Indians from many different nations participate.

One important purpose of the Navajo Nation Fair is to keep alive the Indian traditions and crafts of the past. The following activities can give your children some understanding of how Native Americans lived long ago. Before you begin them, you may want to take a look at the following book.

A New True Book: Indians by Teri Martini, Childrens Press, 1982.

Totem Poles

You will need:

Cardboard tube from bathroom tissue

Wooden craft stick

Scraps of construction paper

Markers, crayons, or paints

Knife

Scissors

Stapler

Pencil

Totem poles were made and are still made today by the Indians of the Northwest Coast. These Indians carved the trunks of tall cedar trees into animal and human shapes. Totem poles are carved as a symbol of family pride, as a memorial to the dead, and even as public "shame" poles when a person in the community has done something wrong.

Here is an easy totem pole the children can make from scraps and recyclables.

1. Every child needs a cardboard tube from bathroom tissue, a wooden craft (popsicle) stick, some scraps of construction paper, and some markers, crayons, or paints.

2. Help the children use a sharp knife to make a vertical slit about 1/2 inch long, 1 1/2 inches down from the top of the tube. When you have cut the slit, continue straight through the tube to cut an identical slit directly opposite. Have the children slip the craft stick through the holes so that it projects equally on either side of the tube.

3. Birds are a favorite Indian symbol, so we use the craft stick to support paper wings. Have the children fold a piece of construction paper in the color of their choice so that it is about 5 inches long along the fold and 1 1/2 inches wide. Then cut it in half, so there are two pieces about 2 1/2 inches long along the fold and 1 1/2 inches wide.

4. On each paper, make a wing as follows. On the first piece of paper, with the folded edge at the top, draw a scalloped line connecting the top right corner with the lower left corner. Do the opposite on the second piece so that the wing tapers from a point at the upper left to the full 1 1/2-inch width at the right. Cut on the lines you've drawn and set the wings aside.

5. Now have the children use crayons, markers, or paints to decorate their "poles." Remember, animal motifs were used extensively on totem poles. Do the children want their totem poles to look fierce or gentle? Is it a totem to honor a family or person or a "shame" pole? Design and color it accordingly.

6. When the pole is colored and dry, place the paper wings over the ends of the craft stick with the fold on top and paper covering both sides of the stick. Staple the wings to the stick.

7. If you plan to do the Indian Villages activity, have the children write their names inside their totem poles and save them to go in their Indian villages.

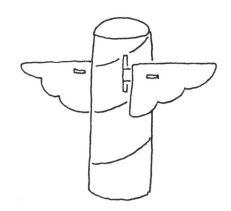

Tepees and Hogans

To make a tepee you will need:

Tan or brown paper or oaktag

Coffee can lid

Pencil

Scissors

Tape

3 or 4 tiny twigs

Crayons or markers (optional)

To make a hogan you will need:

Egg carton

Scissors

Masking tape

Brown paint, marker, or crayon

Indians lived in many different kinds of homes. A tepee made of buffalo skins was home for the Plains Indians. As hunters, these Indians were always on the move, following the buffalo herds. The tepee could be easily packed and set up again.

The name "Navajo" means "takers from the field." The Navajo were farmers who stayed in one place. These Indians built cone-shaped hogans out of timber covered with bark and earth.

Let the children decide if they are hunters or farmers and then build some tepees or hogans.

To Make a Tepee:

1. Have the children trace a circle 4 to 5 inches in diameter on a piece of tan or brown paper or oaktag. (They can trace around a coffee can lid.) Cut out the circle.

2. Cut a wedge shape out of the circle that is equal to about $1/3$ of the circle. Decorate the remaining $2/3$ circle with crayons or markers as you like.

3. Fold the $2/3$ circle into a cone shape overlapping at the bottom edge and leaving a small hole at the top point. This is the smoke hole. Secure the cone where it overlaps with a piece of tape.

4. Cut a vertical slit from the bottom edge of the tepee about halfway up. Fold back the paper on each side of the slit. This is the entrance and the flaps can remain open or closed depending on the weather.

5. Finally, find 3 or 4 tiny twigs, as straight as possible and 2 to 3 inches long. Stick them in the top hole of the tepee so that the tops project out of the hole about 1/2 inch. In a real tepee, these poles would be the framework on which the buffalo skins would be stretched.

To Make a Hogan:

1. Have the children cut one egg cup off an egg carton. This is the basic shape of an old-fashioned Navajo hogan. Now you must add the "bark and earth" covering.

2. Tear off tiny pieces of masking tape and stick them on the egg cup. Overlap the bits of tape until the egg cup is completely covered. Leave one opening on the bottom edge of the "hogan" for an entrance. If there are any other spaces cut out of the egg cup, cover them with tape.

3. Now use brown paint, marker, or crayon to color over the tape. The overlapping tape gives a rough bark texture that is emphasized when you color it.

Let each child make a few tepees or hogans. If you are making an Indian village have the children write their names in their tepees or hogans and save them.

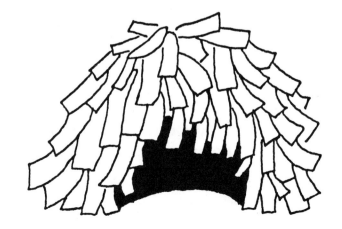

211

Canoes

You will need:

One 3-by-6-inch piece of stiff paper or oaktag

Crayons or markers

Pencil

Scissors

Ruler

Glue

In the Northwest, the Indians carved canoes from logs. Indians of the Northwest built birchbark canoes, which they used for fishing, traveling, and hunting expeditions.

Here is an easy paper canoe the children can make.

1. For each canoe you want to make, you need a piece of stiff paper or oaktag 3 inches wide and about 6 inches long. You can use tan or brown paper or color it yourself.

2. Fold the paper so that it is $1^1/2$ inches wide and about 6 inches long. With the fold on the bottom, mark two pencil lines on the folded edge about $1^1/4$ inches in from each end. Draw curved lines connecting the upper corners of the paper with the marks you drew. These are the curved ends of the canoe.

3. To draw the upper edge of the canoe, first make a pencil mark 3 inches from the side of the paper and 1 inch up from the folded edge. Then draw a shallow "smile" connecting the two upper corners of the paper. The line should cross the pencil mark. The canoe is about 1 inch high in the center.

4. Cut out on the lines you drew. Open the paper and put a line of glue along the edge of each of the four short curved ends. Press together and let dry.

5. When the glue has dried, you can gently bend the paper to open the canoe. The children can make one or more canoes and save them to use in the next activity.

Indian Villages

You will need:

Shallow box or box lid

Stiff cardboard (to reinforce the bottom)

Paints, crayons, or markers

Foil (for water)

Branches, twigs, pinecones, etc.

Clay

Small stones

Red tissue or construction paper

Now let the children put all their creations together in a traditional Indian village.

1. Each child needs a shallow box or box lid. If you use a dress or shirt box, reinforce the bottom with a piece of stiff cardboard.

2. First each child creates the grounds of his or her Indian village. Where is the village—on the plains, along a river, in a forest or a canyon? With paints, crayons, or markers, color in the appropriate ground. Water can be represented in blue or with foil.

3. Add your tepees or hogans and totem pole. If you have canoes, place them in or near the water. Trees can be branches or pine-cones supported in small lumps of clay. Rocks, moss, and sand can also be added.

4. It's fun to add a campfire to the village. Make a ring of small stones. Within the ring, glue small sticks for firewood and crumbled red tissue or construction paper cut into "flames."

5. According to the age and interest level of the children, the villages can be as simple or elaborate as you like. Children of any age can have a lot of enjoyment recreating this tiny scene from Native American history.

Navajo Dry Painting

You will need:

Selection of colored sand
White glue
Gray or tan cardboard
Pencil
Newspaper

For the Navajo, dry painting was not just art. It was a religious ceremony performed by the shaman, or medicine man, to get rid of evil spirits.

Sand was spread on the floor of the hogan to make a smooth background for the painting. The dry "paint" was made of powdered rocks and minerals of different colors. The shaman slowly and carefully added the colored powders by hand to form a picture. As soon as the ceremony ended, the painting was swept away.

The sand paintings described below are more permanent works of art inspired by the Navajo tradition.

1. You will need a selection of colored sand available in craft stores. Each child needs white glue and a piece of cardboard. Gray or tan cardboard works better than poster-board.

2. Let each child draw a simple design on the cardboard. Indian art was inspired by nature, so tell the children to think of natural things to draw (e.g., the sun, moon, or stars, waves of water, birds, bears, deer, corn). Remember, keep the designs bold and simple! It is difficult for artists new to sand painting to work in fine lines or intricate designs, so keep the areas large and well defined.

3. Now it gets messy, so work on newspaper. Have the children fill in one area of the design at a time with glue. Pour the glue on thickly, making the cardboard opaque white. Then sprinkle the desired color sand over the glue to cover it completely. Work slowly and carefully until the entire design is filled in with colored sand. Keep the picture flat to dry several hours or overnight.

4. When the glue is dry, shake off the excess sand. You have a Navajo-style dry painting. However, unlike the originals, yours should last for a long time.

Indian Food

For many Indians throughout the country, corn was the main food. When European settlers came to America, the Indians shared their knowledge of corn with them.

The following recipe may be familiar to the children but they may be surprised to learn that it is really traditional Indian food!

Cornbread

   1 cup yellow cornmeal

   1 cup flour

   2 tablespoons sugar

   4 teaspoons baking powder

   1/2 teaspoon salt

   1/4 cup shortening, softened

   1 egg

   1 cup milk

Blend cornmeal, flour, sugar, baking powder, and salt in a medium-sized bowl.

In a large bowl, blend shortening and egg. Add milk. Then stir in dry ingredients and beat vigorously for at least 1 minute.

Cornbread can be baked in an 8- or 9-inch square pan or as muffins (yields 12 medium muffins).

Pour batter into well-greased pan or muffin tin.

Bake in a preheated 425°F oven. Bread takes 20 to 25 minutes. Muffins will be done in about 15 minutes.

How would the Indians have baked their cornbread?

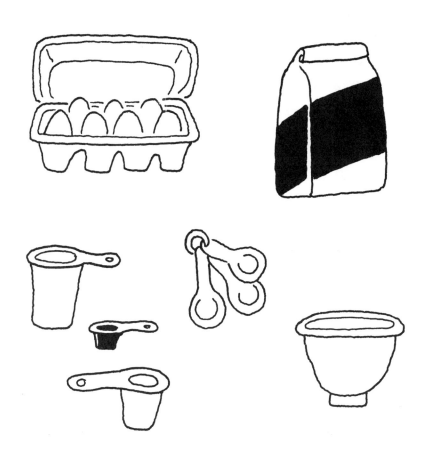

215

SEPTEMBER 23 | Autumnal Equinox

On or about September 23, the sun crosses the equator in its apparent movement from north to south. On the equinox, as its name indicates, day and night are equal. In the Northern Hemisphere, this is the autumnal equinox and autumn begins today.

If September 23 brings autumn where you live, and if autumn brings brightly colored falling leaves, give the next three activities a try. But first, take a look at the following book.

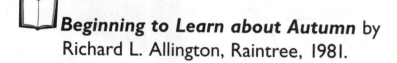 ***Beginning to Learn about Autumn*** by Richard L. Allington, Raintree, 1981.

Autumn Trees

You will need:

> 1 sheet of bright blue construction paper
> Crayons or markers
> Scraps of colored paper—red, orange, yellow, brown
> Glue

One of the most dramatic signs of autumn is the vivid coloring of the leaves. In this craft, the children can enjoy creating their own brightly colored autumn trees.

1. Give each child a sheet of bright blue construction paper. This will be the background of sky. Have the children noticed that some of the clearest blue skies can be seen in autumn?

2. With crayons or markers, have the children draw the ground and a simple tree trunk with a few branches. Don't be too elaborate with the branches since most of them will be covered up.

3. Bring out the scraps of colored paper in red, orange, yellow, brown, etc. Have the children tear off little pieces for leaves. Then let them glue them onto their tree branches. Since this is a fall tree, they can also glue some "leaves" falling down from the tree and some on the ground.

4. When the pictures are dry, display all the different fall trees. They should help you get in the spirit of the season!

Leaf Matching Game

You will need:

2 fallen leaves of each type
Newspaper
Waxed paper
Iron

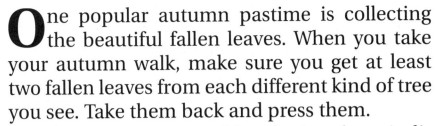

One popular autumn pastime is collecting the beautiful fallen leaves. When you take your autumn walk, make sure you get at least two fallen leaves from each different kind of tree you see. Take them back and press them.

Leaves can be pressed by placing them individually between two sheets of newspaper and then under a stack of heavy books. This method takes about two weeks. To speed up the process you can iron the newspaper-covered leaves. Once the leaves have been pressed by either method, you can make them a little less fragile by waxing them. Lay a sheet of waxed paper on top of the leaf and iron it with a warm iron. Turn the leaf over and repeat on the other side.

Now that you have a collection of pressed leaves, try this activity with the children.

1. Give each child one leaf. Try to have as many different types of leaves as possible.

2. On a table, lay out the rest of your collection. Have the children go to the table one at a time and find a leaf that matches theirs. Obviously, this works best if you have a good-sized leaf collection so that even the last child has to do some searching.

3. Remind the children that they might not find an identical leaf. Their match may be a little smaller or larger and the coloring may be a bit different. They are matching by shape and hopefully by type of tree.

4. When everyone has found their matches, help the children identify the trees their leaves fell from by using reference books. Look under call number 582 in your library for books on trees.

Fall Placemat

You will need:

8 to 10 pressed leaves

One 12-by-18-inch sheet of paper

Two 12-by-18-inch pieces of clear self-stick paper

Rolling pin

Straight pin

Pinking shears (optional)

With some clear self-stick paper and pressed leaves, the children can make a permanent and useful souvenir of the season.

1. Let each child choose 8 to 10 pressed leaves. Have them try different arrangements until they have one that they like within a 12-by-18-inch space. (They can lay their leaves on a 12-by-18-inch sheet of paper, just to get the idea of the dimensions. They will not need the paper for the placemat.)

2. Give each child a piece of clear self-stick paper 12 by 18 inches. Lay it flat on the work area, sticky side up. Carefully place the leaves on the self-stick paper. Remind them to decide where they want each leaf before they put it down. Once it is stuck it is difficult to move it.

3. When all the leaves are on, lay another 12-by-18-inch piece of self-stick on top, sticky side down. This is tricky so help the children with this part. You can use a rolling pin, and if you get any air bubbles prick them with a pin and then press flat.

If you like, you can finish the edges of the placemat by trimming with pinking shears.

Now you can enjoy the colors of fall all year long—whenever you use your one-of-a-kind placemat!

Did you know that Johnny Appleseed was a real person? He was born John Chapman on September 26, 1774, in Massachusetts.

Chapman earned his nickname "Johnny Appleseed" by planting orchards of apple trees from Pennsylvania westward to Indiana. Carrying no gun, the gentle Chapman's respect for the Indians as well as the wild animals, which he refused to hunt, brought him safely through the western wilderness.

To learn more about this fascinating American, read:

Johnny Appleseed by Steven Kellogg, Scholastic, 1988.

Here are some fun apple activities.

Apple Treats

You will need:

Several varieties of apples

Knife

Large pot

Apple juice or water

Cinnamon

Show the children a selection of apples of different varieties. Point out the differences in color and shape. Identify some varieties of apples by their appearance. (Look at the blossom end of a Delicious apple. See the five bumps. If the bottom of your apple has five bumps, you know it's a Delicious apple.)

Cut an apple in half horizontally. (If you think of the apple as a globe, cut it at the equator line.) Show the children the design inside made by the seeds. Help the children cut some "star apples." Then continue cutting the apples into smaller pieces to be cooked into applesauce.

219

Remove seeds and cores. The peels can be left on. Put apple pieces in a large pot. Add enough apple juice or water to cover the bottom of the pot to a depth of about ½ inch. Cover and cook on low heat, bringing to a boil. Stir frequently. Cook until apples soften into sauce. Sprinkle with cinnamon and eat. Your homemade apple-sauce is especially delicious warm.

As you enjoy it, remember Johnny Appleseed.

Apple Trees

You will need:

Red construction paper at least 9 by 12 inches

Brown construction paper

Scissors

Glue

Markers

Green construction paper

Hole punch

1. Give each child a sheet of red construction paper at least 9 by 12 inches. This is the background for the pictures.

2. Let the children cut simple tree trunks (6 to 8 inches tall) out of brown paper. Have them glue the tree trunks onto the red paper, leaving room at the top of the paper for the leafy part of the tree. They can draw in a ground line if they like.

3. Next let each child cut the leafy part of the tree out of green paper. Any irregular, cloud-like shape is fine. It should be all one piece.

4. Let each child use a hole punch to make round holes all over the green tree-top paper. They may need to fold the paper to reach the middle with the paper punch. Have them punch lots of holes.

5. Now let the children glue the tree top at the top of the trunk, overlapping slightly. See all the apples on your tree?

A Friend in Your Apple

You will need:

Cardboard

1 piece of stiff paper or posterboard

Markers or crayons

Pencil

Scissors

Hole punch

Ballpoint pen

Young children really enjoy this craft.

1. On a piece of stiff cardboard, draw the outline of an apple (about 6 inches tall) with a sturdy stem and a leaf or two. Cut it out. The children will use it as a pattern.

2. Have each child trace the apple pattern on stiff paper or posterboard. Let them color it and then cut it out.

3. With a hole punch, make a "worm hole" in each apple. Have each child poke a finger through the hole to make the worm. With a ballpoint pen, draw a happy face on each little "worm."

George Gershwin was born September 26, 1898. He lived in New York and worked as a composer. A composer writes songs and music.

Gershwin wrote many popular songs including "Swanee" and "I Got Rhythm"; however, he is probably most famous for his "Rhapsody in Blue."

The music of "Rhapsody in Blue" seems to be the perfect inspiration for one final apple activity.

Skyline of the Big Apple

You will need:

Recording of "Rhapsody in Blue"

Picture of the skyline of New York

1 sheet of heavy white art paper

Watercolors

Paintbrush

Container of water

Black construction paper

Scissors

Glue

Get a recording of Gershwin's "Rhapsody in Blue" and a poster or photograph of the Manhattan skyline to show the children. Have they ever heard New York City called "The Big Apple"? This nickname came from the slang of jazz musicians. In jazz slang, an "apple" is a city, so New York is the "Big Apple."

Now get out your watercolors and turn on the music. With a little inspiration from Gershwin, we will create our own views of the Big Apple.

1. Give every child a sheet of heavy white art paper, some watercolors, a paintbrush, and a container of water. Have the children dip their brushes in the plain water and paint it all over their art paper.

2. Now with a very wet paint brush, let the children paint a sunrise sky filling the entire paper. They can use red, orange, pink, purple, blue, even green. They can drip water on the painted surface for different effects or blot the painted surface with tissues. When the sunrise is finished to their satisfaction, set it aside to dry.

3. Bring out the black construction paper and scissors. Have the children cut out some skyscraper silhouettes. Just cut rectangles of various widths and heights. (You can top one with a triangle for the Empire State Building.) Arrange them on top of the sunrise painting, using the bottom edge of the painting as the ground line. When you are satisfied with the arrangement, glue them on.

4. Display these sunrise skylines in honor of the birthday of that famous and talented New Yorker, George Gershwin.

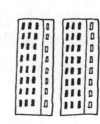

Good Neighbor Day

The Good Neighbor Day Foundation of Lakeside, Montana has declared the fourth Sunday in September every year to be National Good Neighbor Day.

A Neighborly Visit

Are there any people in your neighborhood who could use a visit?

Shut-ins and residents of nursing homes or adult day care centers often get great pleasure from a visit with children.

Call ahead to establish a convenient time and then plan what you will do during your visit. You can entertain your neighbors with a few songs, or play some card games or board games. Most of all you can be prepared to listen. Sometimes the best gift we can give our neighbors is a listening ear, and often what we hear is fascinating. Children can get some firsthand accounts of history from their elderly neighbors. You may be surprised at how much you receive when you give a little time to your neighbors.

When we pay a neighborly call it's nice to bring something to share. The following activity has a recipe you can make together and take with you on your neighborly visit.

A Neighborly Treat

Gingerbread is especially delicious when served warm and can be topped with a spoonful of applesauce.

This is a delicious and easy-to-make dessert that seems especially good at this time of year.

Gingerbread

4^1/$_2$ cups flour

^{2}/$_3$ cup sugar

2 cups dark molasses

1^1/$_2$ cups hot water

1 cup shortening

2 eggs

2 teaspoons baking soda

2 teaspoons ginger

2 teaspoons cinnamon

1^1/$_2$ teaspoons salt

Preheat oven to 325°F. Grease and flour a 13-by-9-by-2-inch baking pan.

Measure all ingredients into a large bowl and stir to blend. Beat for about 3 minutes. Pour into pan and bake for about an hour. Gingerbread is done when a wooden pick inserted in the center comes out clean.

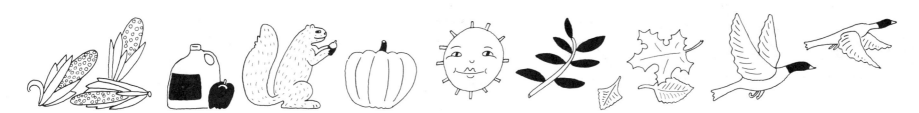

OCTOBER

One dark night, when I was tucked in bed,
Mrs. O'Leary left the lantern in the shed
And when the cow kicked it over,
she winked her eye and said
"They'll be a hot time in the old town tonight
Fire! Fire! Fire!"

There is a bit of truth in that old song. The Chicago Fire of October 9, 1871, did begin in the O'Learys' barn but no one knows exactly how it started. We do know that before it was over almost one-third of the people in Chicago were left homeless.

The anniversary of the great fire became the first Fire Prevention Day. Today in the United States and Canada, Fire Prevention Week is held annually in the week including October 9.

To learn more about fires and fire prevention, read aloud the following book to the children. Then take a look at the following activities.

Fire! Fire! by Gail Gibbons, Thomas Y. Crowell, 1984.

"Fire" in Sign Language

The sign for "fire" looks like rising flames.

Hold both hands, palms facing the chest, with four fingers and thumb separated and extended pointing up. Wiggle the fingers while moving the hands in upward alternating circles (first right hand goes up, then left, etc.)

A Fire Experiment

You will need:

Candle

Small candle holder

Matches

1 small glass jar

1 medium glass jar

1 large glass jar

With a candle, some matches, and three glass jars—one small, one medium, and one large—the children can learn an important fact about fire.

1. Secure the candle in a holder and light it.
2. Cover the candle with the small jar turned upside down. As soon as you cover it, begin counting with the children. What happens to the candle? Write down the number to which you had counted when the candle went out.
3. Relight the candle and repeat step two with the medium-sized jar and then the large jar, counting each time.

Did you count a little higher each time before the candle went out?

4. What does this experiment teach us about fire? Help the children draw their own conclusions by asking the following questions.
   –Why did the flame go out each time we covered the candle?
   –Why did the flame burn longer as we increased the size of the jars covering it?
   –What is inside the jars?

Now take the knowledge you just discovered and use it in the following fire prevention exercise.

Stop, Drop, and Roll

In the previous activity, the children verified for themselves the fact that fire needs air to burn. In this activity, they can learn an effective way to stop a fire from getting the air it needs to go on burning.

1. Have the children run from one side of the room to the other. Point out to them that the faster we move, the more we can feel the air rushing against us (blowing our hair or our clothes).

227

2. Imagine with the children that you are caught in a fire. Your clothes catch on fire. Your first instinct might be to run away. But we have just seen that when we run, the air rushes against us and that would feed the fire and make it grow. So stop! Do not run. The first step in putting out the fire is STOP!

3. DROP! Fall on the ground and lie down, arms and legs straight. This is the second step in putting out the fire. Drop to the ground.

4. Now with your arms and legs straight, roll along the ground. You are smothering the fire against the ground, cutting off its air supply. Step 3 to put out the fire is ROLL!

5. Practice STOP, DROP, AND ROLL with the children. Hopefully, with enough practice, the children will automatically remember to STOP, DROP, AND ROLL if they ever need to.

Fire Safety Posters

You will need:

1 piece of drawing paper or posterboard
Crayons or markers

Creating your own fire safety posters can be an enjoyable way to reinforce these lifesaving instructions.

1. Give every child a piece of drawing paper or posterboard and some crayons or markers.

2. Each child should choose one fire safety principle that they would like to illustrate. Here are some examples:
   –Never play with matches. If you find matches, give them to a grown-up.
   –Do not touch anything on the stove.
   –Keep papers and rags out of the attic or basement. They are a fire hazard.
   –If your clothes catch on fire—STOP, DROP, AND ROLL.
   –On a picnic or cookout, do not play near the campfire or grill.
   –Do not play with electrical plugs or outlets.
   –Learn the fire emergency telephone number.
   –Plan fire escape routes at home and practice them with fire drills.

3. Let or help the children write a fire safety caption. Then let them illustrate it.

4. When the posters are finished, display them and look at each one. Talk about the fire safety principles illustrated.

What European explorer was the first to sail across the ocean and "discover" America? Some people think that almost five hundred years before Columbus arrived, Norwegian Vikings, led by Leif Ericson, came.

In 1964, a presidential proclamation declared October 9 to be Leif Ericson Day. On this day, Norwegian-Americans throughout the country hold celebrations in honor of this brave explorer.

To learn more about Leif Ericson read:

Explorers of America: Leif Ericson by Dan Zadra, Creative Education, 1988.

The explorers who set out to discover new lands were equipped with weapons, and protective shields and helmets. The following two activities show the children how to make their own distinctive Viking helmets and shields.

A Viking Helmet

You will need:

Posterboard (cardboard)
Scissors
Stapler
Tape
Newspaper
Aluminum foil

Although we often see pictures of Vikings wearing a horned helmet, most Viking helmets were simple cone-shaped caps of leather or metal, sometimes with a straight nosepiece down the front. This is the type of Viking helmet we will make out of posterboard and aluminum foil.

1. Let each child measure a piece of posterboard 28 by 2 inches and cut it out. Let the children help each other wrap the strips of posterboard around each other's heads. These strips will be the bottom edges of the helmets. Overlap the posterboard to fit around the head and staple together. Cover the staple with a little tape so it doesn't scratch. When fitting the helmet edges, don't make them too tight. Our helmets will be covered with foil, so leave the posterboard slightly loose to allow room for the foil.

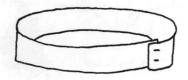

2. Next have the children cut another strip of posterboard 20 by 1½ inches. This piece will attach to the back of the helmet edge and go over the top of the helmet and down beyond the front edge, creating a nosepiece. Some pictures show Viking helmets pointed at the top. If you want a point at the top of the helmet, bend a crease in this cardboard strip at the top of the helmet. When the children have helped each other fit this second piece of cardboard onto the first, they can attach it with staples at front and back. The end of the nosepiece can be cut into a triangular, arrow-shaped point. Again, cover all staples with tape.

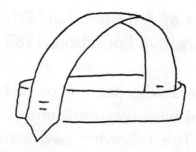

3. Now you have a skeleton framework for the helmets. Before covering with foil, have the children crumple newspaper into a ball. Put the ball of newspaper in the helmet to give a temporary head shape to it.

4. Now give each child 2 pieces of aluminum foil about 20 inches long. Have them lay one on top of the other, dull sides together, shiny sides out. Connect the two pieces by folding them together at one long (20 inch) side. Fold the edges over 1/2 inch and then again another 1/2 inch. Then open the foil shiny side to you.

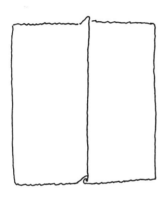

5. Drape the foil over the helmet framework so that the folded seam is perpendicular to the nosepiece. Fold the foil under the cardboard, creating the skin over the helmet skeleton. Trim excess foil as necessary. Don't worry about keeping the foil smooth. It will look like hammered metal when you are finished.

Now that your Vikings' heads are protected, how about making shields?

A Viking Shield

You will need:

Corrugated cardboard

Scissors

Silver duct tape

Brown crayons

Ruler

Pencil

2 brass paper fasteners

Viking warriors carried small, round, wooden shields. An iron bar across the back held the wood boards together and also served as a handle for the shield. Sometimes shields were trimmed with iron rims around the edge. Although a metal shield would have provided greater protection for a warrior, it would have been too heavy to wield effectively.

With some corrugated cardboard, the children can make replicas of Viking shields.

1. On a piece of corrugated cardboard, have each child trace a large circle. (We traced a 16-inch pizza pan.) Let or help the children cut out the circles.

2. Cover the cut edge of the circle with silver duct tape (available in hardware stores), letting the tape overlap on both sides of the edge. This is the iron rim of the shield.

3. Let the children use brown crayons to make their shields look like wood. Have them feel the cardboard to see which way the ridges go. In line with the ridges, have the children draw four or five brown lines from one edge of the circle to the opposite edge. This divides the shield into "boards." Then, using an unwrapped brown crayon, rub it along the cardboard varying the pressure from light to heavy. The irregular rubbing pattern simulates the wood grain. Color both sides of the shield in this way.

4. Have the children use a ruler to measure another piece of corrugated cardboard about 2 inches wide and almost the length of the diameter of their shield. Cut it out. This is the "iron bar/handle" of the shield. Cover it completely with silver duct tape.

5. Lay the "bar" across the shield so that it dissects the circle at a right angle to the "boards." Attach it by poking a hole about 1 inch in from each end of the "bar" and through the shield. Insert a brass paper fastener in each hole so that the heads of

the fasteners are on the front of the shield and the stems come through the handle. When they are bent in place, cover the stems with small pieces of silver duct tape.

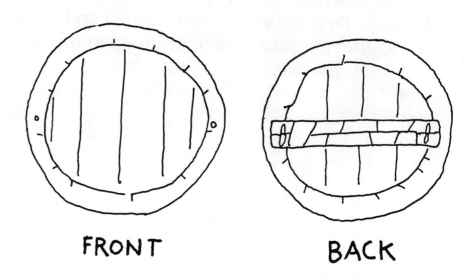

FRONT   BACK

When you wear your Viking helmet and carry your Viking shield, remember Leif Ericson and his fellow explorers who set sail in search of new lands one thousand years ago.

The great American actress Helen Hayes was born on this day in 1900 in Washington, D.C. Hayes began her acting career at the age of five, and for the next sixty years she performed on stage, radio, film, and television and won many awards.

Act It Out

You will need:

Paper

Pencil

Box or jar

1. On small slips of paper, print out single words that each describe some expressive emotion. For example:

    ANGRY—SAD—HAPPY—EXCITED— SURPRISED—FRIGHTENED—WORRIED

    You can also include expressive physical states such as:

    SLEEPY—STRONG—WEAK

2. Fold the paper slips and put them in a box or wide-mouth jar.

3. One at a time, let each child reach in, pick out a slip, and "act it out" until everyone else can guess the word.

    Can you spot any future stars of stage and screen?

Young children may enjoy:

The Berenstain Bears Get Stage Fright by Stan and Jan Berenstain, Random House, 1986.

On this day in 1884, Eleanor Roosevelt was born. Her uncle, Theodore, was the 26th President of the United States. When she grew up, Eleanor married her cousin Franklin Delano Roosevelt, who became our 32nd President.

Eleanor took her job as First Lady seriously and became a strong champion of people who needed help. After her husband died in 1945, Eleanor Roosevelt was appointed delegate to the United Nations. She has been called the First Lady of the World.

As a United Nations delegate, Eleanor Roosevelt was in charge of the Human Rights Commission. Under her leadership, this commission created a Universal Declaration of Human Rights, describing the rights to which every person in the world is entitled.

Honor the birthday of this great champion of human rights by creating . . .

Your Own Declaration of Human Rights

You will need:

Large posterboard   Group of friends
Marker

1. At the top of the poster print: "Every Person on Earth Has a Right To:"
2. Now share some ideas with your friends. What do you think every human being on earth is entitled to?

   Here are a few ideas to get you started:
   - Enough food to be healthy
   - The right to think as you please and say what you think
   - A roof over your head
   - The right to believe what you want
   - An education
   - A safe place to live
   - Clean air to breathe
   - Clean water to drink
   - The right to publicly disagree with your government
3. As each new idea is expressed, the "author" can write his or her idea on the poster.

Young people spending her birthday thinking about human rights is probably just the kind of celebration Eleanor Roosevelt would like best!

Count Kazimierz Pulaski was a Polish nobleman who led a cavalry corps against the British in the American Revolutionary War. He died from battle wounds here in America on October II, 1779.

By presidential proclamation the date of his death has been declared Pulaski Day. Many American cities, including New York City, hold parades and celebrations in honor of this Polish hero of the American Revolution.

A Polish Greeting

First, find Poland on a globe or a world map. What countries are Poland's neighbors? Where is Poland in relation to your location? What route might you travel to get there?

Pulaski Day is a special day for Polish-Americans. In honor of the day, help the children learn a Polish phrase of congratulations or good wishes.

Sto Lat! (pronounced *stoh* to rhyme with snow—*lot)*

Sto Lat translates, "May you live one hundred years!"

Born October 16, 1758 in Hartford, Connecticut, Noah Webster was a teacher, a journalist, a lawyer, and an author. To most of us, however, he is best remembered as the lexicographer who gave us *The American Dictionary of the English Language,* our first American dictionary.

Celebrate Noah Webster's birthday with the two dictionary activities below.

Different Kinds of Dictionaries

You will need:

Different kinds of dictionaries

Are the children aware of the many different kinds of dictionaries available?

Gather a collection of different kinds of dictionaries and let the children browse. You may want to include:

- Picture dictionaries
- Children's dictionaries (much more inclusive than picture dictionaries but simpler than adult dictionaries)
- A multivolume adult dictionary
- Foreign language dictionaries (be sure to include some with different characters, i.e., Russian, Japanese, etc.)

- Sign language dictionaries
- Dictionaries of specialized fields, e.g., music, art, etc.

What do all the dictionaries have in common?

Learn a New Word

You will need:

Paper

Pencil

Scissors

Large jar

Several dictionaries

What better way to honor Noah Webster than by "looking it up"?

1. According to the age level of the children in your group, write out a selection of words that you think will be new to them. (Write out more words than you have children.) Cut the words out individually, fold up the papers, and put them in a big jar.

2. Let each child reach into the jar and pick out a word. Direct the child to the appropriate level dictionary to look up the word. He or she can write down the definition or just remember it.

3. Let everyone share a new word and its meaning with the group. In this way, you can all learn quite a few new words today!

If you have older children in your group, how about including "lexicographer" in your word jar!

Young children will enjoy the following book.

I'll Teach My Dog 100 Words by Michael Frith, Random House, 1973.

Today is the anniversary of the day in 1945 when the United Nations was created.

It was established to keep peace, encourage cooperation between nations, and protect human rights throughout the world. Since 1948, the President of the United States has proclaimed October 24 to be United Nations Day, a day to appreciate and celebrate the many different cultures in our world.

You Are a U.N. Representative

You will need:

Encyclopedia

Simple props to represent different countries

In honor of United Nations Day, just for today, you are the U.N. Secretary-General and your group is the general assembly. Each child is a United Nations delegate from a different country.

1. Have the children pick country names out of a hat so each child gets a different country to represent.

2. The children have two jobs. First, they should each learn a little bit about the country they represent. (Young children can learn one fact or find the country on the world map or globe. Older children can use the encyclopedia to learn a little more.)

Second, the children each need one prop to symbolize the country they represent. The Mexican representative may wear a sombrero, the Colombian representative may carry a can of coffee, etc.

3. Now come together again as a group. As Secretary-General, call upon the representatives one at a time to stand up and share something about their countries.

4. When everyone has spoken, you probably will all have learned something new about the many countries in our world. You will also be ready to relax and enjoy the next activity.

United Nations Feast

You may be surprised at the ethnic diversity in the backgrounds of the children in your group. Even if the children are all American-born, their ancestry will probably include many different cultures.

For this activity have the children bring a food to share that reflects their own ethnic background. (Remember, the choice may not match the last name. Some children are more familiar with their mothers' cultural traditions and foods than their fathers'.)

If the food is homemade from a family recipe, encourage the children to work with their parents to prepare the dish. That way, they can share how it is made.

If no one at home is available to cook, keep it simple. Pretzels can represent Germany, tortilla chips from Mexico, rice from China, and bananas from Brazil.

Prepare a table to hold the food and label each dish with the country of its origin. You can even add little flags for each country.

Encourage the children to try different foods. Sampling new foods from countries other than our own is an enjoyable way to get a taste of the many cultures in our world.

Are the children surprised at the cultural diversity in your own group? The following book offers a light-hearted look at cultural diversity.

Come Over to My House by Theo. LeSieg, Random House, 1966.

The great magician and escape artist, Harry Houdini, died on October 31, 1926. In his honor, it has become a tradition for magicians to meet on this day, and October 31 every year is observed as National Magic Day.

Remember the famous magician today with a read-aloud of the following book:

📖 **The Houdini Box** by Brian Selznick, Knopf, 1991.

Then take some time to learn a little magic!

Learn a Magic Trick

You will need:

Newspaper

Scissors

Magicians often amaze us by turning ordinary objects into something new and different. Even very young children can make a tall tree grow out of a newspaper by following these instructions.

1. Take a full sheet of newspaper (two pages if you were reading it), and fold the top edge to meet the bottom. Cut on the fold line.

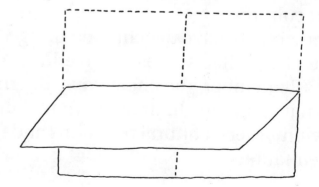

2. Roll one piece into a tube until there is about 5 inches left on the end. Overlap the other piece and continue rolling into the tube.

3. Flatten one end of the tube. On the flattened end, cut down from the top end about 4 inches. Make 4 of these 4-inch cuts.

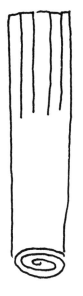

4. Holding the uncut end (the trunk of the tree) in one hand, reach in with the other hand and gently pull the "leaves" upward to make the tree "grow."

5. Older children can use more than two pieces of paper. It's a little harder to cut, but the tree will be much taller.

Your library has children's books on magic tricks shelved under call number J793.8. Why not check out a few so that any aspiring magicians in your group can pursue the subject further. Who knows, you may inspire another Houdini!

"**S**amhain," a very old Celtic holiday, means "summer's end." On this day, people thanked the sun god for the summer that had just passed and made offerings to the lord of the dead. It was believed that on Samhain night the ghosts of the dead were allowed a short visit among the living before the cold winter to come. Many of today's Halloween customs are based on the spirit of Samhain.

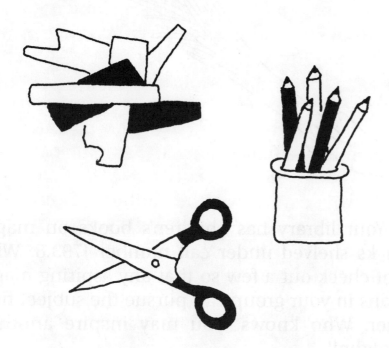

Ghostly Windsocks

You will need:

White paper
Markers or crayons
Pencil
Scissors
Glue
White crepe paper
Hole punch
Stapler
String

Samhain was thought to be a night for ghostly visitations. Here is a ghost the children can make and display in the "spirit" of the day.

1. Give each child a piece of white paper about 18 inches across and about 12 inches long. In the middle of the paper, have the children draw a ghostly pair of eyes and a mouth with crayons or markers.

2. On another piece of white paper trace each child's hands, including about 2 inches of wrist on each hand. Have the children cut these out.

3. On either side of their ghost faces, have the children attach their two hands, gluing only on the wrist parts so that the hands stick out.

4. Turn the ghost over and on the reverse side glue about 6 crepe paper streamers hanging down from the bottom edge of the white paper.

5. Punch two holes near the top edge of the ghost and about 5 inches in from the sides. (You may want to reinforce these two holes with tape.) Now staple the two sides of the ghost together, overlapping slightly, forming a cylindrical wind sock. Tie a piece of string (at least 24 inches long) with one end in each hole.

6. The children can hang their ghostly wind socks outside their homes as a welcome to any Samhain visitors who may stop by!

Samhain Lanterns

You will need:

Large turnip or squash
Sharp paring knife
Awl or large nail
3 pieces of string—30 inches each
Small tea candle
Matches

Fire was an important Samhain symbol. Tremendous bonfires were lit, and the glowing coals from these fires were carried in hollowed out turnips or potatoes. These "lanterns" were also thought to light the way for the wandering spirits who were abroad on Samhain.

Older children can carve their own lanterns in remembrance of the ancient Samhain custom.

1. You can carve the lanterns from large turnips or any squash in season in your neighborhood. Have the children carefully cut the tops off their vegetables and then hollow them out. They will need to be careful not to cut through the sides or bottom.

2. Next, with a sharp paring knife, cut a design in the sides of the vegetable. Unlike a jack-o'-lantern, this doesn't have to be a face. You can cut out any abstract design that light can shine through.

3. When the designs are cut out, have the children each poke three holes at equal distances close to the top edge of the vegetable. A large nail or an awl works well for making holes. Cut three pieces of string or twine about 30 inches each. Thread each string through a hole and pull the 2 ends even at the top. Tie the 6 ends together in a knot at the top.

4. Give each child a small tea candle. (A taller candle will burn the string.) Have them put the candles in their "lanterns" and carefully light up. Turn out the lights to get the full effect of your "Samhain lanterns."

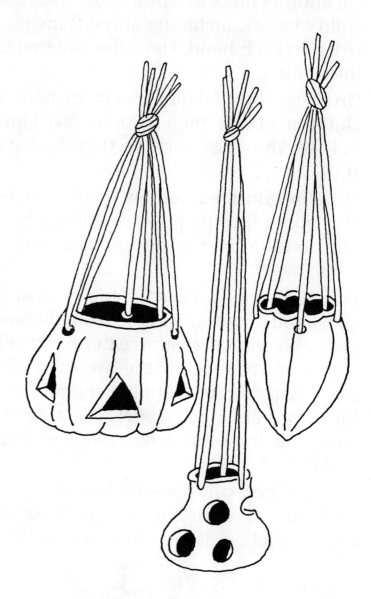

OCTOBER IS NATIONAL POPCORN POPPIN' MONTH

The Popcorn Institute of Chicago has proclaimed October to be the month "to celebrate the wholesome, economical, natural food value of popcorn, America's native snack."

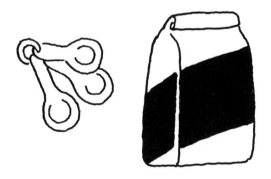

Delicious Popcorn Treats

Popcorn is certainly delicious all by itself or with a little salt or butter. However, if in honor of National Popcorn Poppin' Month, you feel a little more adventurous, try these two variations on an old favorite.

Cinnamon Delight Popcorn

Ingredients

- 3 tablespoons butter or margarine
- 2 tablespoons sugar
- 1/2 teaspoon cinnamon
- 2 quarts popped popcorn

1. In a small pan, melt butter or margarine over low heat. Add sugar and cinnamon and stir until sugar is dissolved.

2. Put popcorn in a bowl or can that has a snug-fitting lid. Drizzle butter mixture over popcorn. Cover and let everyone take a turn shaking the popcorn.

3. When the popcorn has been tossed enough to coat it thoroughly—enjoy!

Peanut Buttery Popcorn

Ingredients

1½ tablespoons butter or margarine
1½ tablespoons peanut butter
1½ tablespoons honey
2 quarts popped popcorn

1. In a small pan, over low heat, melt butter or margarine. Blend in peanut butter and honey, stirring over low heat until mixture is blended and liquid consistency.

2. Put popcorn in a bowl or can that has a snug-fitting lid. Drizzle butter mixture over popcorn. Cover and let everyone take a turn shaking the popcorn until it is thoroughly coated.

As you sample your popcorn treats, take a look at the following book.

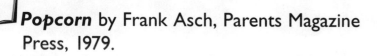 *Popcorn* by Frank Asch, Parents Magazine Press, 1979.

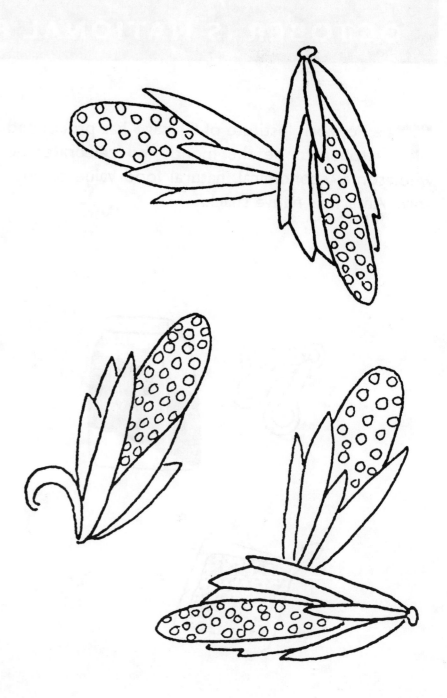

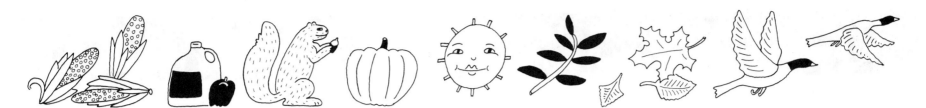

November

In the United States, general elections are held on the first Tuesday following the first Monday in November. On this day, presidents, senators, representatives, governors, and state and local government officials are elected. Although in the past only white men who owned property were allowed to vote, today any American citizen eighteen years or older has the right to vote.

Help the children understand the election process better with a read-aloud of the following book.

A New True Book: Voting and Elections by Dennis B. Fradin, Childrens Press, 1985.

Exercise Your Right to Vote

You will need:

"Ballot box" with slit in the top
Paper
Large piece of paper for tally

Even though the children are too young to vote in the general election, they can still exercise their right to vote today.

1. First, select your "candidates." We suggest vanilla and chocolate ice cream. Let the children vote for their favorite.

2. For a truly free election, you need secret ballots. Place a covered ballot box with an open slot in the top at the front of the room. Older children can simply write "vanilla" or "chocolate" on a slip of paper, fold it, and drop it in the ballot box.

Younger children can be given preprinted ballots with either the words "vanilla" and "chocolate" or pictures of vanilla and chocolate ice cream cones. Each child can circle his or her choice, fold up the ballot, and drop it in the ballot box.

3. When everyone has voted, tally the votes. You may want to make a chart and mark strokes under the appropriate "candidate" as the votes are counted. Then declare the winner.

4. Once the winner is elected by a majority, everyone lives with the results. So get ready to serve the winning ice cream. When should you enjoy the results of your election? How about on Inauguration Day!

"Win" and "Lose" in Sign Language

~~~~~~

At election time, banners, bumper stickers, and signs appear just about everywhere. Here are two more "signs" of the time you may enjoy learning.

The sign for "win" mimics the action of grabbing for a trophy.

Hold the left hand in a fist with the thumb over the curled fingers. The left hand is held in front of the body. The right hand with fingers and thumb extended, palm facing left, sweeps down from the right side of the body to the top of the left hand. As the right hand moves toward the left, the fingers close into a fist matching the left hand.

The sign for "lose" depicts the action of dropping or "losing" what you have.

Hold both hands in a "C" position, four fingers curving together and thumbs curving up toward the fingertips.

Face both palms toward the chest, knuckles facing each other and touching. Bring your hands downward and apart, letting the fingertips drop down.

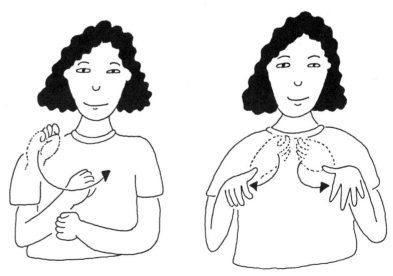

More than two hundred years ago, a gambler figured out a way to enjoy his meal without interrupting his card game. The gambler was the English nobleman, John Montague, the Fourth Earl of Sandwich, and the meal he invented is named for him. John Montague was born on November 3, 1718, and in his honor November 3 has been designated "Sandwich Day."

Invent a New Sandwich

Convenient to carry and easily enjoyed just about anywhere, the sandwich is truly a wonderful invention. If the children in your group think a sandwich has to be some meat or peanut butter and jelly between two slices of bread, the following activity should broaden their vision of possibilities!

1. First, enlist the children's help in providing a wide selection of sandwich fixings.

   "Breads" could include rye, pumpernickel, pita, tortillas, rice cakes, quick breads such as banana bread or date nut, sourdough, rolls, bagels, etc.

   Vegetables—you can include more than lettuce and tomatoes in a sandwich. How about sprouts, shredded carrots, pickles, crisp raw zucchini, etc.

Fruits can be a tasty part of a sandwich. Try some raisins, sliced bananas, sliced strawberries, pineapple, etc.

For the protein element of the sandwich, other than meat, try all different kinds of cheeses as well as cream cheese, peanut butter, and other nut butters or ground nuts sprinkled on top of something else, hard-cooked eggs and even tofu or refried beans.

Condiments can include butter or margarine, ketchup, mustard, mayonnaise, salad dressings (Italian, ranch, Russian, thousand island), or jam.

2. Set up a big table with the breads at one end and then all the fillings. Encourage the children to try new combinations of foods in their sandwiches.

3. When each child has made a sandwich, you may suggest that it be cut in quarters so that friends can sample it.

4. Have the children talk about the sandwiches they invented. Do they like the taste of them? Not every new creation will be a success but you can't tell until you try!

5. As you enjoy your culinary creations, take a moment to remember their originator, John Montague, Earl of Sandwich.

Tutankhamen was pharaoh of ancient Egypt while he was still a boy and died before he was twenty. In keeping with Egyptian customs, when Tutankhamen died in 1352 B.C., he was buried with many valuable possessions, which were to serve him in his afterlife.

On November 4, 1922, the archaeologist Howard Carter discovered the hidden tomb of Tutankhamen. The tomb had not been disturbed for the more than three thousand years since the boy-king had been buried. The treasures found within this tomb have greatly enriched our understanding of ancient Egypt.

For a better understanding of the historical detective work archaeologists like Howard Carter do, see:

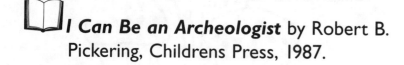 *I Can Be an Archeologist* by Robert B. Pickering, Childrens Press, 1987.

Egyptian Hieroglyphics

You will need:

Drawing paper
Pencil

How did Howard Carter know whose tomb he had discovered? The name of Tutankhamen was inscribed throughout the tomb in hieroglyphics.

Hieroglyphics are writings in which words or sounds are each represented by a picture or symbol. Although some Egyptian hieroglyphics represent a whole word, most of them represent a sound, similar to our alphabet.

 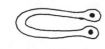   

Like the Egyptians, we can create our own hieroglyphic writing.

1. First have each child make a chart of his or her own hieroglyphic alphabet. Like the Rosetta Stone of ancient Egypt, this chart can be used to decode the hieroglyphic messages you write.

   On their charts the children should each write the 26 letters of our alphabet. Next to each letter, have them draw a simple picture or symbol representing a word that begins with that letter. The key here is to keep the symbols extremely simple, since you will be drawing them many times to spell out your messages. Here are some examples: apple for A, ball for B, can for C, dot for D, egg for E, etc. If you get stuck for ideas, look at a picture dictionary.

2. Once they have created their hieroglyphic alphabets, let the children try them out. Young children can write out their names. Older children can write messages.

   Egyptian hieroglyphics were written vertically or horizontally, so take your pick.

3. When the messages are completed, hang them up and try to decode them. Only refer to the alphabet charts as a last resort.

  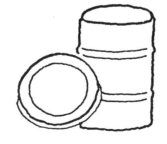 

William Penn Adair Rogers was born on this day in 1879 in Oologah Indian Territory (now Oklahoma). Rogers became famous for the funny stories he told while performing rope tricks on the New York stage. Even though he often made fun of the leaders of his time, Will Rogers once remarked that he never met a man he didn't like.

Lassos

You will need:

> 6 to 7 feet of rope

Will Rogers was great at fancy trick roping. Without long practice, we can't get too fancy but we can learn one basic technique of cowboy roping—lassoing.

The word "lasso" is from the Spanish "lazo," a word meaning "snare." In this activity the children can learn to make a lasso knot called a "honda" and then practice some roping.

1. For each child provide 6 to 7 feet of rope. (We used cotton clothesline. You do not want stiff plastic rope.)
2. Help the children tie a honda knot (see illustration) about 6 inches from one end of the rope. Then between the honda knot

and the short end of the rope, tie a simple overhand knot. This knot is used as a "stopper" to keep the rope from slipping out of the loop of the other knot.

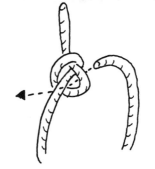

3. Let the children make the loops of their lassos very big so that the tail of the rope left over is only a few inches long. The bigger the loop, the easier it will be for them to lasso something.

4. Before any roping begins, stress to the children that they must only try to rope inanimate objects (doorknobs, table and chair legs, cones, etc.).

As you try your roping skills remember, the cowboys had to rope running steers while they were riding horses!

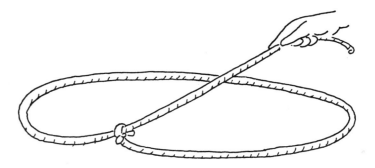

This English holiday originated with an assassination attempt almost four hundred years ago. The Gunpowder Plot of November 5, 1605 was a plan to kill King James I of England by blowing up the room in which he was to meet with Parliament. Guy Fawkes was the man who was to light the fuse, setting off the explosion. The plot was exposed and Fawkes and his fellow conspirators were hanged.

Guy Fawkes Day is celebrated with fireworks and bonfires on which straw figures called "guys" are burned.

Locate England on a globe or world map. What countries are England's neighbors? Where is England in relation to where you live? What route might you travel to get there?

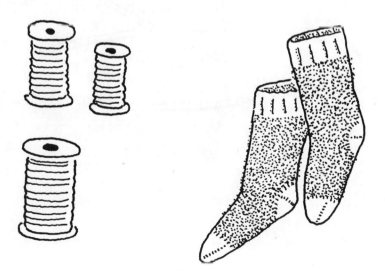

Make a "Guy"

You will need:

Old pair of pantyhose
Old button-down shirt
Old pants
Twine
Paint
Hat (optional)
Straw or newspapers
Scissors

Did you know that the slang word "guy" originated with Guy Fawkes?

To commemorate the British holiday, why not work as a group to make a "guy."

1. You will need an old pair of pantyhose, an old button-down men's shirt, men's pants, and some twine. (The shirt and pants should be cast-offs. They will not be wearable again.) You will need paint to make your guy's face. A hat is optional.

Like our American scarecrows, guys are traditionally stuffed with straw. However, if this is not available, newspaper will work just as well.

2. Let some children work on the guy's head. Tie a knot in the pantyhose at the top of the legs. The panty part will be the guy's head. Stuff it with straw or crumpled newspaper until it is tightly packed, leaving just enough room to tie off the "waist" at the top of the head. The empty legs of the pantyhose will be used to attach the head to the torso of the guy.

   With paint, create a face for the guy. You can paint on hair. Then when the paint is dry, attach the head to the torso.

3. Let some children work on the guy's torso. First have them cut 4 to 6 holes near the bottom edge of the shirt. You will use the holes in attaching the torso to the legs. If the pants have belt loops, position the holes in the shirt to correspond with the loops.

   Lay the shirt unbuttoned on the ground. Position the head in place above the shirt and lay one leg of the pantyhose down the inside back of the shirt. Tie off the wrists of the shirtsleeves with twine. Stuff the sleeves with straw or crumpled newspaper.

Then stuff the body of the shirt. After stuffing it full, position the other leg of the pantyhose over the stuffing and button up the shirt. Tie the bottoms of the two pantyhose legs together to help hold the stuffing in the torso.

4. Let a third group of children work on the legs of the guy. Tie off the ankles of the pants with twine. Then stuff the pants tightly with straw or newspaper.

5. Now attach the top of the guy to the bottom. If the pants have belt loops, thread short lengths of twine through the holes you poked in the shirt and then through the belt loops and tie tightly. If the pants do not have loops, poke holes near the waistband to correspond to the holes in the bottom of the shirt and connect with twine.

Display your guy so that everyone will:

"REMEMBER, REMEMBER
THE FIFTH OF NOVEMBER
GUNPOWDER, TREASON AND PLOTS;
I SEE NO REASON WHY
GUNPOWDER TREASON
SHOULD EVER BE FORGOT."

NOVEMBER 6 | John Philip Sousa's Birthday

The next time you hear a stirring march played by a brass band, think of John Philip Sousa. Born on November 6, 1854, Sousa wrote about 140 marches including his most famous, "The Stars and Stripes Forever." Sousa served as bandmaster of the U.S. Marine Band for twelve years and later led his own popular band, which toured the United States and Europe. John Philip Sousa certainly earned his title, "The March King."

To learn more about this talented American read:

📖 *John Philip Sousa: The March King* by Carol Greene, Childrens Press, 1992.

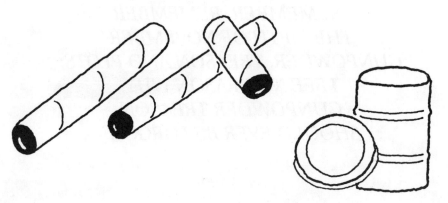

A Marching Band

You will need:

Tape of Sousa's "Stars and Stripes Forever"
Empty coffee cans with lids
Rulers or spoons
Pot lids
Blocks
Sandpaper
Cardboard tubes
Stapler

A long with his many other accomplishments, John Philip Sousa invented a brass wind instrument called the sousaphone. Today you can use objects around you to "invent" musical instruments. Then cooperate to form a marching band. Here are some suggestions.

Drums—Empty coffee cans covered with plastic lids. (If you made the stilts in the Circus Stilts activity, you have two drums complete with strings to hang around your neck.) Rulers or spoons make good drumsticks.

Cymbals—Two pot lids

Rhythm sticks—Two blocks

Rhythm scratchers—Staple sandpaper around two blocks. Rub them against each other.

Tambourines or maracas—See the Maracas activity

Clarinets or flutes—Take the cardboard tubes from paper towels or bathroom tissue. Poke a few holes in a line. Now use your voice to "toot" your clarinet or flute while moving your fingers over the holes.

Add anything else you can use to make music.

Now get a tape of John Philip Sousa's "Stars and Stripes Forever." Pick up your tape player, have the children pick up their instruments, and march!

This rousing activity is a great way to celebrate the birthday of John Philip Sousa!

Born today in 1887, Georgia O'Keeffe was an American artist with a distinctive and dramatic style. She is most famous for her desert landscapes and her close-ups of flowers.

Show the children some prints of O'Keeffe's flowers. Point out the vivid colors and simple forms. Also notice how each flower fills the canvas and even overflows it.

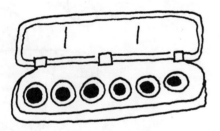

Fantastic Flowers

You will need:

A few real flowers
Paper
Watercolor paints

1. Provide each child with paper and watercolors and some real flowers to observe closely. Have each child choose one flower to paint. Let him sit near the flower to get a close-up view.
2. You don't need pencils because you aren't concerned about details. Keep colors vivid and dramatic and most of all, make sure the flowers fill (or overflow) the paper. Leave little or no empty space.
3. When the paintings are dry, exhibit them and spend Georgia O'Keeffe's birthday surrounded by the kind of fantastic flowers she painted so well.

If you have children ages three, five, or seven in your group, this is their special holiday. In Japanese, "Shichi Go San" means "seven five three." On Shichi Go San, every November 15, Japanese parents give thanks for their sons who have reached the ages of three or five and for their daughters who have reached the ages of three or seven. Dressed in their best clothing, the children visit a shrine with their family. There thanks are given and blessings are asked for a long and healthy life for these children. The children bring long, narrow paper bags to the shrine, which their parents fill with goodies. For Japanese children, three, five, and seven are wonderful ages to be!

If you haven't already done so, locate Japan on a globe or world map. To learn more about Japan that celebrates Shichi Go San, take a look at the following book.

A New True Book: Japan by Karen Jacobsen, Childrens Press, 1982.

Japanese Treat Bags

You will need:

12-by-15-inch piece of white freezer wrap
Ruler
Pencil
Glue or tape
Scissors or pinking shears
Markers or crayons

The treat bags Japanese children are given on Shichi Go San are long and narrow and beautifully decorated. If you can find plain, long, narrow paper bags such as those used for wine or French bread, get one for each child in your group. Then refer to step 5 to learn how to decorate your bags the traditional Japanese way.

If you can't find the bags already made, the children can make their own using the following instructions.

1. Give each child a piece of white freezer wrap 12 by 15 inches. Have the children lay the paper waxy side up and 15 inches vertically, 12 inches across.

2. Have the children fold the sides of the paper in toward the middle, about 2½ inches on both the right and left sides.

3. Now unfold the paper and turn it over so that the papery side is up and it is positioned 15 inches horizontally. From the top fold line, measure down ¾ inch and put 3 to 4 pencil dots to mark the measurement. Lay a ruler along those marks and fold the top of the paper up along the edge of the ruler. Turn the paper over, waxy side up, and fold again, accordion-style. You are making the pleat in the side of your bag. When it is finished, turn the paper so that the folds you just made are at the bottom of the paper and follow step 3 again to make the pleat in the other side.

4. The long open edges of the bag should overlap. Glue or tape them together. Then fold the bottom of this paper tube up about 1 inch and then over again. Tape to close the bottom of the bag. The children can use scissors to cut the top edge into a curved or zigzag edge or use pinking shears. You should now have a bag about 4 inches wide and about 12 inches long.

5. Traditional symbols of youth and long life are used to decorate the treat bags. Have the children use markers or crayons to draw turtles, pine trees, and cranes (any big bird will do) on their bags. Then see the following activity for some ideas on filling the bags.

Shichi Go San Treats

~~~~~~

You will need:

Thin bamboo skewers
Mini-marshmallows
Presweetened fruit-flavored "O" cereal

One of the traditional treats that Japanese parents put in their children's bags on Shichi Go San is a long pink sugar candy called *chitose ame* (pronounced chee-to-say ah-may). You can certainly go to an Asian grocery and purchase Japanese candy. However, we think young children will enjoy making the following sweet treats for their bags.

1. You will need thin bamboo skewers available in kitchen supply stores or Asian grocers. Have several for each child. You will also need mini-marshmallows and presweetened fruit-flavored cereal shaped like "O"s.

2. Give each child a few skewers, a container of marshmallows, and a container of cereal. Let them thread marshmallows and cereal on their skewers, completely filling them. (If you wet the skewers first, the marshmallows slide on easily without tearing.)

3. Have the children begin and end with a marshmallow to hold the cereal on. In between, they can thread any combinations they like. You might let each child make three, five, or seven skewers in honor of the day. What they don't enjoy right away, they can slip into their beautiful bags to save for later.

NOVEMBER 18 | Louis Daguerre's Birthday

Louis-Jacques-Mandé Daguerre was born near Paris on November 18, 1789. When he was already a successful painter, Daguerre worked with a French scientist to perfect the first permanent photographs in 1839. These images on metal plates became known as "daguerreotypes" and led to today's photographs.

So the next time someone tells you to say "cheese," remember, this photo moment was brought to you courtesy of Louis Daguerre!

For books on this subject, check your library shelves under call number J770.

Photographic Fun

You will need:

Camera
Film

What better way to remember Louis Daguerre on his birthday than by taking some pictures! It's hard to wait for results, so if possible, use an instant camera for this activity. If you must wait for film to develop, try to get it back within a day or two, so the experience of taking the pictures will be fresh in the children's minds as they look at the finished products.

Very young children may have never used a camera before. Here are some tips you may want to share with them.

1. What you are photographing is called your "subject." It can be a person or group of people but it doesn't have to be. Your subject can be the view outside your window or a still life of interesting objects.

2. What you see through your viewfinder is exactly what you will get in your photograph—so look closely and carefully.

3. Since this is an exercise for beginners, keep it simple. Center your subject.

4. Check your background. Is there anything there you don't want in your photograph? If there is, remove it. (Remember step 2.)

5. A common mistake beginning photographers make is not getting close enough to the subject. When you think you have set up your shot just right, take two steps closer.

6. If the camera moves as you take the picture you will get a fuzzy image. So when you are ready, hold your breath and push the button.

7. Display your photographs with credit given to the photographers.

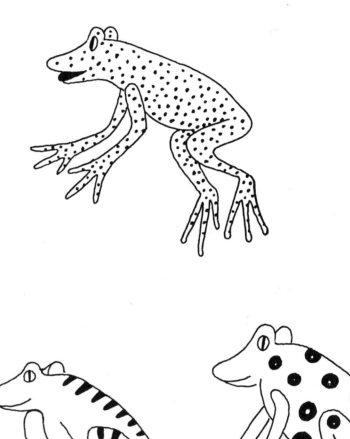

The National Council for Adoption has set aside this week every year to celebrate the success of adoption.

Learn About Adoption

This is the week to help the children in your group understand that there is more than one way that families happen. With stories and discussion, you can clear up some common misconceptions about adoption and point out its positive aspects.

The National Council for Adoption specifies three kinds of adoption: infant, intercountry, and special needs. These three kinds of adoption certainly overlap and the following stories talk about them.

Infant

Susan and Gordon Adopt a Baby by Judy Freudberg and Tony Geiss, Random Books/Young Readers, 1992.

Intercountry

We Adopted You, Benjamin Koo by Linda Walvoord Girard, Albert Whitman, 1989.

Special Needs

Usually when we hear "special needs" we think of children who are physically or psychologically challenged. However, in adoption, age becomes a "special need." Older children are much harder to place with adoptive families than infants. The following book deals with both the special needs of a child no longer an infant and an intercountry adoption.

Through Moon and Stars and Night Skies by Ann Turner, Harper & Row, 1990.

Are there any children in your group who were adopted? Would they or their parents like to share their experiences with the group? If not, do you know any adoptees of any age who can speak to your group and answer the children's questions? The best way for other children to really understand adoption is for them to be able to talk openly with someone who was adopted.

If you can make only one point clear to the children this week, let it be this one.

Adoption is just another way a child becomes part of a family. Once a legal adoption is completed, the status of the adopted child is exactly the same as that of a biological child.

Adoption is forever.

Samuel Clemens's (Mark Twain) Birthday

Printer, newspaper reporter, steamboat pilot, Confederate soldier, and silver miner, Samuel Langhorne Clemens led a rich and exciting life. He wrote about many of his experiences under the name "Mark Twain." ("Mark twain" is a riverboat term for two fathoms or twelve feet deep, a safe depth for the riverboats.)

Some of Mark Twain's more famous works include *The Adventures of Tom Sawyer, The Adventures of Huckleberry Finn,* and *A Connecticut Yankee in King Arthur's Court.*

On November 30, 1835, the night Samuel Clemens was born, Halley's comet appeared in the sky. On April 20, 1910, Halley's comet made its next appearance and a few hours later Samuel Clemens died.

Two good juvenile biographies of Samuel Clemens are:

Mark Twain, Author of Tom Sawyer by Carol Greene, Childrens Press, 1992.

Mark Twain? What Kind of Name Is That? by Robert Quackenbush, Prentice Hall, 1984.

Frog Jumping Contest

You will need:

Piece of blue paper or foil for a pond
Tiddlywinks (counting chips)
Markers
White correction fluid

The first book of Mark Twain's to be published was a collection of short stories called *The Celebrated Jumping Frog of Calaveras County and Other Sketches.*

In honor of the author's birthday, why not hold your own "frog jumping" contest?

1. You will need some open floor space, with the children on the floor around the edges.
2. You will need a "pond" in the center of the open space. A piece of blue paper or foil cut in a pond shape is perfect.

3. Your "frogs" are tiddlywinks (round flat counting chips or flat buttons work fine). Give each child one chip to be the frog. The children can even paint eyes on their frogs (a dot of white correction fluid with a black dot of marker in the center makes a great eye). The children also each need another chip to make their frogs jump.

4. Position the children around the edges of the open floor area at an equal distance from the pond. When you say "go" let the children use their chips to make their "frogs" jump toward the pond. The first to land in the pond is the winner and can earn the title of Celebrated Jumping Frog of your county!

   When all the jumping is finished consider settling down with a read-aloud of Mark Twain's story, "The Celebrated Jumping Frog of Calaveras County."

DECEMBER

It may be the winter where you are, but for the half of the world in the Southern Hemisphere it's summer! Show the children the Southern Hemisphere on a globe and then have fun working together on a summer collage.

Summer Collage

You will need:

Long piece of computer paper

Markers

Old magazines

Real seashells

Sand

Scissors

Glue

1. Get a big, long piece of computer or printer paper—big enough for all the children to work on comfortably.

2. On the paper, outline the word "SUMMER" in big, fat letters that fill the page. The letters must be big. Our collage materials will go inside them.

3. Lay the paper out on the floor.

4. Let the children cut or tear summery pictures from old magazines and glue them within the letter outlines. Let them add real seashells and sand sprinkled on the glued paper.

5. Display your summer collage to beat those midwinter blues. Remember, it's summer in the lands down under!

Born on this day in 1859, Georges Seurat was a French painter. The painting technique he is famous for is called pointillism. In pointillism, instead of mixing paints to shade the colors, the artist fills the canvas with tiny dots of pure, unmixed colors and lets the viewer's eyes blend them.

The most famous pointillist painting is Seurat's *A Sunday Afternoon on the Island of La Grande Jatte*. Show a copy of this painting (illustrated in almost every art history book) to the children. Then let them try their own hands at pointillism with the next activity.

A Pointillism Project

You will need:

I sheet of white paper
Paints
Cotton-tipped swabs
Pencil

1. Every child needs a sheet of white paper, paints, and some cotton-tipped swabs.

2. First let the children outline a simple picture lightly in pencil on their papers. Some ideas are a few flowers, fish, a butterfly. Pointillism is time-consuming so don't try anything too detailed or elaborate.

3. Now fill in the drawing with small dots of color applied with the cotton swabs. Remember, do not mix colors. Older children can simulate shading by using dots of darker color in areas that are turning away from the viewer, and light colors in areas turning toward the viewer. Fill in the entire picture, including the background, with dots of color.

4. When the paintings are dry, display them and stand back. Your eyes can only mix the dots of color from a distance.

There are probably not many children in the world today whose lives have not been colored by the man whose birthday we celebrate on December 5. Walter Elias Disney was born on this day in 1901 in Chicago. From Mickey Mouse to *The Lion King*, the Disney company has created thousands of animated films. Millions of tourists come every year to visit the Disney theme parks and meet the many characters Walt Disney introduced to the world. In fact for most of us, "Disney" means wonderful family entertainment.

For more biographical information on Walt Disney see:

The Man Behind the Magic: The Story of Walt Disney by Katherine Barrett and Richard Greene, Viking, 1991.

Easy Animation

You will need:

At least 16 small sheets of paper
(index cards work well)
Markers
Stapler

In the kind of animation Walt Disney made famous, every action in the film is created by using a series of drawings, each one just slightly different than the last. The drawings are photographed and when played in fast sequence, an illusion of movement is created.

We can get a better understanding of this kind of animation by doing some ourselves. A flip book is an enjoyable exercise in animation.

1. Each child needs at least 16 small sheets of paper. A stiff paper works best—even index cards can be used.

2. Let each child choose a simple action sequence to draw and animate. Here are some suggestions: a bouncing ball, a shooting star, a falling leaf, a bud opening into a flower, an insect flying, etc. You can even draw a stick figure and make it move.

3. Draw all the pictures at the far right of the paper. On the first sheet of paper draw the beginning situation in the action sequence, e.g., a tightly closed bud. On the last sheet draw the end of the action sequence, e.g., a fully opened flower. Then count out to page 8 and draw a picture of the situation at the halfway point in the action sequence—a half-open flower.

4. Now fill in pages 2 to 7 and 9 to 15 with the appropriate pictures—each one just slightly different than the one before. Be sure to position the pictures on the papers so that their placement corresponds to the one before and after.

5. Stack the sheets, tapping the stack to line the paper up as perfectly as possible. Staple along the left margin to "bind" your flip book.

6. Using your thumbnail along the right edge of the book, flip the pages quickly and watch your drawings come alive. You can even run the "film" backwards by starting on the last page and flipping to the first.

Now that you've seen how long it takes to create simple animation, just imagine the job Disney animators have in creating a feature-length animated film, which uses over one million drawings!

DECEMBER 6 St. Nicholas Day

St. Nicholas was a bishop who lived in Asia Minor (now Turkey) in the fourth century. Known for his charity, after his death Nicholas became the patron saint of children. December 6, the anniversary of St. Nicholas's death, is a holiday in Europe on which children who have been good receive gifts. When Dutch settlers in America continued the tradition of celebrating St. Nicholas Day, they called the saint by the Dutch name "Sinterklass." In time this evolved into Santa Claus.

A lovely book about St. Nicholas is:

A Gift from Saint Nicholas by Carole Kismaric, Holiday House, 1988.

St. Nicholas Staffs

Every picture of St. Nicholas shows him in his bishop's vestments. On his head he wears the tall pointed hat called a miter. He carries a crozier, or shepherd's staff, the symbol of the bishop's authority as the shepherd of his flock.

In honor of St. Nicholas we can make tasty pretzel snacks in the shape of a shepherd's staff.

Ingredients

2 tablespoons yeast

1 cup warm water

2 teaspoons honey

2 teaspoons salt

2½ cups flour

1 egg

Dissolve yeast in warm water. Add honey and salt and stir to blend. Add flour. Knead on floured surface until dough is smooth.

Break dough into small balls (1 to 2 inches in diameter). Roll balls into thin pencil shapes about 6 inches long. Curve one end to make a bishop's staff. Lay staffs on baking sheets.

Brush staffs with an egg that has been beaten with 1 teaspoon water. Sprinkle with salt and bake at 425°F for 10 minutes. (Makes about 2 dozen staffs.)

In keeping with the generous spirit of St. Nicholas, share your pretzels with some friends.

Although St. Lucia was Italian, her feast day is a popular holiday in Sweden where it marks the beginning of the Christmas season. In Swedish villages on this day, children parade down the streets wearing special costumes and carrying cake and coffee to homes, hospitals, and businesses of the town.

Locate Sweden on a globe or world map. What countries are Sweden's neighbors? Where is Sweden in relation to where you live? What route might you travel to get there?

The following activity shows how to make a simple version of St. Lucia Day crowns for girls and hats for boys.

Crowns and Hats

To make a girl's crown you will need:

One 6-by-28-inch piece of white posterboard
Scissors
Ruler
Pencil
Green tissue paper
Glue
Markers
Stapler

To make a boy's hat you will need:

One 26-by-13-inch piece of white posterboard
String
Pencil
Ruler
Glue
Silver or gold glitter
Stapler

277

Girls' Crowns

On St. Lucia Day in Sweden, only the oldest daughter in each home wears the traditional white robe and crown of green garland and candles. In the village procession, one girl is chosen to represent St. Lucia. In your group, however, every girl can make a St. Lucia crown to wear.

1. Give each girl a piece of white posterboard 6 by 28 inches. Let the girls help each other measure the posterboard around their heads. Leaving about a 3-inch overlap, cut off the excess length.

2. Have the girls measure up from the bottom of the posterboard about $2^1/_2$ inches and draw a line at this height across the posterboard. The space within this $2^1/_2$-inch strip will become the green leafy wreath of the crown.

3. Give each girl two sheets of green tissue paper. Have them tear the tissue into small pieces and glue them onto the posterboard to make the green wreath. Completely cover the $2^1/_2$-inch strip of posterboard with tissue, except for a couple of inches at either end. Leave these plain for the final fitting of the crowns.

4. The $3^1/_2$-inch space above the green wreath is for the traditional seven candles. At the center point of the posterboard, draw a simple lighted candle as tall as the posterboard. (If you draw the candles about an inch wide, they will stand up better.) Then draw three identical candles on either side of the first, spacing them evenly. Leave the candles white but color the flames.

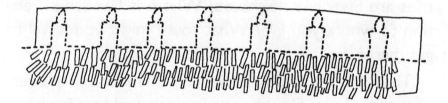

5. When the glue on the wreath is completely dry, cut out the space between the candles. Fit the wreaths and staple them together. If any part of the wreath is bare, cover it with green tissue.

Boys' Hats

In St. Lucia Day processions in Sweden, boys sometimes wear tall cone-shaped hats, beautifully decorated with stars. Let the boys in your group make their own traditional hats with the following instructions.

1. Give each boy a piece of white posterboard about 26 by 13 inches. On it, have him draw a half circle with a diameter of 26 inches. Here is an easy way to make the half circle. Tie a piece of string to a pencil so that the string hanging from the pencil is 13 inches long. Mark a pencil dot at the halfway point (13 inches) of the long side of the posterboard. Get a friend to hold the end of the string on that point. Keeping the pencil perpendicular to the paper and the string taut at all times, swing the pencil around to draw a half circle. Then cut out the half circle.

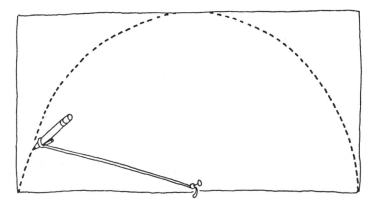

2. Have the children use glue and silver or gold glitter to decorate the half circle with stars. Let glue dry completely.
3. Roll the half circle into a cone, overlapping until there is a point at the top. Staple together.

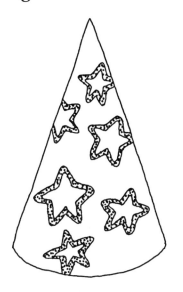

You may choose to wear your crowns and hats in a procession today. You can even deliver goodies to some neighbors as the Swedish children do on St. Lucia Day.

To get a good idea of a child's life in Sweden, see:

Children of the World: Sweden, photography by Tamiko Bjener, Gareth Stevens, 1987.

In the Northern Hemisphere, the winter solstice is the shortest day (and the longest night) of the year and begins the winter season. If December 22 brings winter in your neighborhood and your winter is cold, try the next four activities.

Keeping Warm in Winter

Visit your furnace. Discuss the kind of fuel used. If your furnace has filters, check them to see if they're clean. Clean filters save energy.

Feel the air vents or radiators.

Look at the thermostat and discuss what it does. Lowering it slightly saves energy.

Buildings use oil, gas, coal, wood, etc., as fuel for warmth and energy.

People use food. Food is people fuel. Vegetables are excellent people fuel because they are plentiful and easily converted into energy. In winter, a nice hot bowl of vegetable soup can keep people warm and give us energy.

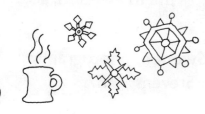

People Fuel—Vegetable Soup

Ingredients

1 large onion

20 cups water

1 (18 ounces) can tomato paste

1 bay leaf

1 tablespoon salt

1 tablespoon sugar

2 envelopes instant beef broth

1 pound stew beef

3 stalks celery

4 or 5 carrots

2 (10 ounce) boxes frozen lima beans

1 (10 ounce) box frozen green beans

1 (10 ounce) box frozen corn

1 can (1 pound) cream-style corn

1/2 cup barley

1. Chop onion into small pieces.
2. Bring water, tomato paste, onion, bay leaf, salt, sugar, and beef broth to a boil in a large pot. Remember, put a lid on the pot to save energy—it will boil faster.
3. Cut stew beef, celery, and carrots into small pieces. Add to the pot and cook for 1 hour or more.
4. Add limas, green beans, corn, cream-style corn, and barley. Simmer 15 minutes or more.
5. Enjoy!

While the soup is simmering, you may like to read the following story.

Stone Soup by Ann McGovern, Scholastic, 1968.

281

Anytime Snow

You will need:

Soap flakes (not detergent)
Small twigs, pinecones, stones, etc.
Small figures, cars, trucks, etc.
Sponge

If Mother Nature doesn't cooperate, we can make our own snow—indoors!

In a big bowl mix 2 parts soap flakes with 1 part water. Mix thoroughly with a wire whisk.

Spread your "snow" on table tops. Add small twigs, pinecones, stones, etc., to make a landscape. Small figures, cars, trucks, etc., can be added to the scene.

When the children are finished, put all the toys in a bucket of plain water and rinse clean.

Children may enjoy cleaning the table tops with a sponge "snow plow" rinsed out thoroughly and squeezed almost dry.

📖 **Katy and the Big Snow** by Virginia Lee Burton, Houghton Mifflin, 1943.

"Snow" in Sign Language

To make the sign for "snow" in sign language, wiggle your fingers and move your hands down like falling snow.

You might like to read the following story aloud, encouraging the children to make the sign for "snow" whenever you read the word "snow."

📖 **Snow** by Roy McKie and P. E. Eastman, Random House, 1962.

Remember Our Feathered Friends

You will need:

Pinecone

Smock or apron

3-foot piece of string or gift tie

Jar of peanut butter

Butter knife

Shallow pan

Birdseed

Waxed paper

Explain to the children that, although many birds fly south for the winter, many stay. When snow covers the ground, it is especially hard for these birds to find food. We can help.

1. Give each child a pinecone and a smock or an apron. This is messy.
2. Give each child a long (about 3-foot) string or piece of gift tie. Help the children tie it around the flat end of the pinecone, leaving two long ends of string. (See illustration.)
3. Put out a jar of peanut butter and butter knives and let the children coat their pinecone with peanut butter.
4. Pour birdseed into a shallow pan. Let the children roll their peanut-buttered pinecones in the seeds until they are all seed-covered.
5. Wrap the pinecones in waxed paper, winding the string around the outside of the waxed paper to keep them wrapped.
6. Tell the children to let a bigger person at home help them hang their bird feeders from a tree branch—near a window if possible—so that everyone can watch the birds enjoy their treat.

Who else might enjoy our bird feeders?

The Big Snow by Berta and Elmer Hader, Collier Books, 1948.

The poem "A Visit from St. Nicholas" was created as a Christmas gift by a father for his children. Clement Clarke Moore wrote the poem for his six children in 1822. One year later, a friend of the Moore family sent it in to the local newspaper, where it was published anonymously on December 23, 1823. Today, "A Visit from St. Nicholas" remains an enduring Christmas classic.

Many beautiful editions of this poem exist, both under its original title and slightly revised under the title "Twas the Night Before Christmas." Here is one that retains the original title and language.

A Visit from St. Nicholas by Clement Clarke Moore, McGraw-Hill, 1968.

A Read-Aloud "Play"

You will need:

Copy of "A Visit from St. Nicholas"
Simple props

Depending on the age of the children, you or one of them can narrate "A Visit from St. Nicholas" while the other children act it out.

The cast is flexible in number. You need two or more "children," Mama, Papa, and St. Nick. You can also add a mouse and eight reindeer.

You can use a few simple costumes (a nightcap, slippers, a Santa hat, etc.) and props (pillows, stockings, small toys, a sack and pipe for Saint Nick, etc.).

By taking part in the action, the children will get an understanding of the poem that they might not have by just listening to it.

Born on this day in 1821, Clara Barton's selfless and courageous nursing during the American Civil War earned her the name "Angel of the Battlefield." After the war ended, she worked to establish and was then appointed the first president of the American Red Cross in 1882. Over a hundred years later, the American Red Cross is still providing aid to victims of disaster both in war and in peacetime.

First Aid Kits

You will need:

Small box with lid (check box)

White paper

Red marker

Soap

Adhesive bandages of varying sizes

Antiseptic wipes or antiseptic spray

Sterile gauze

Sterile tape

Sterile cotton balls

One of the things Clara Barton did that the American Red Cross still does today was to provide medical first aid to those who needed it. In honor of Clara Barton's birthday, help the children make very basic first aid kits.

Talk to the children about "first aid." As the name says, this is the on-the-spot, basic medical attention we give a sick or hurt person as soon as possible. It does not take the place of a doctor's treatment.

1. Give each child a small box with a lid. (Bank check boxes are a good size.) Let the children cover the boxes with white paper and then draw a big red cross on the lid of the box. The red cross is the symbol for first aid.

2. As you pass out each remaining item talk about when and how it might be used.

   When the children have assembled their kits, talk about where they will keep this kit—in their homes, family cars, bike bags, or backpacks. Remind young children that in a medical emergency they should always seek the help of an adult they know and trust!

285

Kwanzaa

This week-long holiday was established in 1966 by Maulana Karenga, a professor of Pan-African studies. The word "kwanzaa" is Swahili for "first" and stands for the first fruits of the harvest. Kwanzaa is a celebration of the traditions and culture of African Americans and makes use of many symbols from African harvest festivals. Each of the seven days of Kwanzaa focuses on a different principle of living.

Kwanzaa is not a religious holiday and is not celebrated by African Americans in place of Christmas or Hanukkah. It was established in the last week of the year so that those who celebrate it will begin the new year inspired and renewed by their traditional values.

Learn more about this interesting holiday with the following:

Kwanzaa by Deborah M. Newton Chocolate, Childrens Press, 1990.

Kwanzaa by A. P. Porter, Carolrhoda Books, 1991.

A Kwanzaa Mkeka

You will need:

One 12-by-18-inch sheet of black construction paper

One 12-by-18-inch sheet of red construction paper

One 12-by-18-inch sheet of green construction paper

Ruler

Scissors

Clear self-stick paper

The celebration of Kwanzaa is rich in symbols, and one important symbol is the "mkeka," or woven tablemat. The mkeka represents history upon which everything else rests.

The children can weave paper mkeka placemats by following these instructions.

1. Give each child three sheets of 12-by-18-inch construction paper, one black, one red, and one green. These colors are also symbolic. Black stands for black people united, red symbolizes the struggle for freedom and equality, and green represents the hope of the future.

2. Let each child choose one paper as the background upon which he will weave the other two colors. Have him fold this paper in half so that it measures 6 by 18 inches.

3. Starting about 1 inch in from the right side, have the children cut straight slits up from the folded edge to about 1 inch from the cut edge. Cut the slits about 1 inch apart, continuing until about 1 inch from the left edge. Now open the paper again.

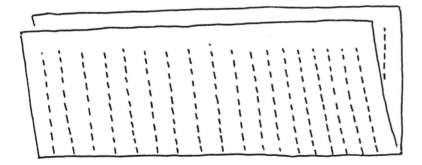

4. From their other two colored papers, have the children cut strips to weave into the first paper. Using rulers, let them cut the strips about 1 inch wide by 18 inches long. They will need 3 to 4 strips of each color.

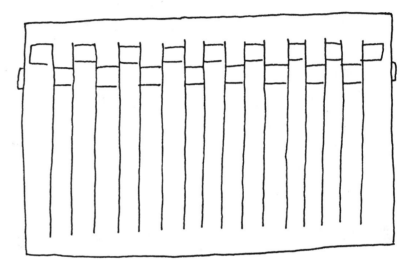

5. Now let the children weave the strips into the background paper alternating colors. (If the first strip starts over the background, then the second should begin under, etc.) Push the strips close to each other so there are no gaps until the mkeka is complete.

6. If you like, you can protect the mkekas by covering them with clear self-stick paper. You can use them as placemats for your Kwanzaa Karamu (feast).

Kwanzaa Muhindi

You will need:

Cardboard

6-inch-long piece of ³/₄-inch-wide gift tie
(gold or tan color)

Stapler

Scissors

Different kinds of dried beans, peas, etc.

Glue

Adhesive-backed magnet

Children are a very important part of Kwanzaa since it is through the children that the African American culture will continue. "Muhindi" is Swahili for "corn" and corn is the Kwanzaa symbol for children. Here is a muhindi decoration the children can make for Kwanzaa.

1. From scrap cardboard, let each child cut a thin oval "corncob" shape about 3 inches long.

2. Give each child a 6-inch-long piece of ³/₄-inch-wide package ribbon in a gold or tan color. This is their cornhusk. Have them fold it at about the center point, forming a "V" and staple the point of the "V" to the top of the "corncob." Trim the ends of the ribbon at an angle.

3. The corn displayed at Kwanzaa is often colorful Indian corn, so for the corn kernels use a mixture of different kinds of dried beans, black-eyed peas, unpopped popcorn, etc. Glue these on to completely cover the cardboard corncob and the stapled part of the ribbon.

4. When the glue has dried completely, add a magnet to the back of the muhindi. (Craft stores sell rolls of adhesive-backed magnet tape that works well.)

5. During Kwanzaa "zawadi," or gifts, are given. Homemade gifts are especially prized. Perhaps the children can give their "muhindi" magnet to someone they love. The "muhindi" can be displayed on refrigerators or any metallic surface.

A Kwanzaa Karamu

There is a "Karamu," or feast, on December 31, the sixth day of Kwanzaa. Everyone brings some food to share and the meal is arranged on the mkeka.

Work together to make the following recipe. (An adult should do the actual cooking.) Perhaps the children can each bring in one ingredient or a beverage to share with the group.

Corn Fritters
Ingredients

I can whole kernel corn

Milk

1 1/2 cups flour

1/4 cup cornmeal

2 teaspoons baking powder

1/2 teaspoon salt

I beaten egg

Oil for frying

1. Drain the corn, reserving the liquid in a 1 cup measuring cup. Add enough milk to the liquid to equal 1 cup. Set aside.
2. Mix flour, cornmeal, baking powder, and salt until blended.
3. Add corn liquid, beaten egg, and corn to dry ingredients. Stir until blended.

4. In a skillet, heat 1/2 to 1 inch of oil until it is hot. (You can test to see if the oil is hot enough by dropping a tiny bit of the corn fritter batter into it. It should sizzle and fry golden brown very quickly.)

Drop the corn fritter batter into the oil by large spoonfuls. Fry until golden brown on both sides.

5. Drain cooked corn fritters on paper towels. This recipe makes 18 to 24 fritters. Serve with pancake syrup. Don't forget to use your mkeka placemats!

It may be difficult to believe, but another calendar year ends today. The Memories activity will help you ring out the old year. The Noisemakers activity will help you ring in the new.

Memories

You will need:

Drawing paper
Markers or crayons

Talk with the children about the year that is ending tonight. Think back on some of the experiences you've shared together and encourage them to remember experiences they have had on their own or with friends or family.

After you've thought and talked for awhile, let each child choose one memory that he or she considers the most memorable moment of the past year.

Let young children draw pictures of their memorable moments. If they want you to, you can write a caption they dictate below the picture. Older children can also draw a picture or they may choose to write about their memorable moments.

Some memories may be private and do not have to be shared with the group. If any child wants to share a memory, invite him to do so. In any event, let the children take their memory projects home and suggest that they date them and tuck them away in a safe place. Then after a few years pass, they can look back and remember all over again.

Noisemakers

You will need:

Clean, empty soda can

5 pennies

Masking tape

Aluminum foil

Stickers

It's fun to ring in the new year with lots of noise. Here is a noisemaker you can make and use for your midnight celebrations.

1. Every child needs a clean, empty aluminum soda can.
2. Let the children put about 5 pennies in their cans and then cover the opening on top with masking tape.
3. Give each child a piece of aluminum foil and have him or her cover the can completely with the foil. Then add a few bright stickers to decorate.
4. When midnight comes, shake your noisemakers to say goodbye to the old year and hello to a brand new year.

And remember, tomorrow you can turn back to page one and enjoy this book all over again!

ACKNOWLEDGMENTS

We'd like to thank our families for their constant support; Amy Teschner for her enthusiasm and vision; Mary Jones for her creative illustrations; and Loraine Page and Pat McIntyre for their interest and advice.

Thanks also to the many talented teachers and library staff who taught our children and inspired us.

And our greatest thanks goes to the many wonderful children we have worked with who have brought our ideas to life.